Liberty and the News

James Madison

THE JAMES MADISON LIBRARY IN AMERICAN POLITICS

Sean Wilentz, General Editor

The James Madison Library in American Politics of the Princeton University Press is devoted to reviving important American political writings of the recent and distant past. American politics has produced an abundance of important works—proclaiming ideas, describing candidates, explaining the inner workings of government, and analyzing political campaigns. This literature includes partisan and philosophical manifestos, pamphlets of practical political theory, muckraking exposés, autobiographies, on-the-scene reportage, and more. The James Madison Library issues fresh editions of both classic and now-neglected titles that helped shape the American political landscape. Up-to-date commentaries in each volume by leading scholars, journalists, and political figures make the books accessible to modern readers.

The Conscience of a Conservative by Barry M. Goldwater

The New Industrial State by John Kenneth Galbraith

Liberty and the News by Walter Lippmann

The Politics of Hope and The Bitter Heritage: American Liberalism in the 1960s by Arthur M. Schlesinger, Jr.

Liberty and the News

Walter Lippmann

With a new foreword by **Ronald Steel**

and a new afterword by **Sidney Blumenthal**

PRINCETON UNIVERSITY PRESS
PRINCETON AND OXFORD

Published by Princeton University Press, 41 William Street,
Princeton, New Jersey 08540
In the United Kingdom: Princeton University Press, 3 Market Place,
Woodstock, Oxfordshire OX20 1SY
All Rights Reserved

First published 1920
First Princeton paperback edition, 2008

Library of Congress Control Number 2007932924
ISBN 978-0-691-13480-2
British Library Cataloging-in-Publication Data is available

This book has been composed in Sabon with Helvetica Neue and
Didot display

Printed on acid-free paper. ∞

press.princeton.edu

Printed in the United States of America

10 9 8 7 6 5 4 3 2 1

Contents

General Editor's Introduction

For more than fifty years, Walter Lippmann was the most respected political journalist in the United States. In 1914, when he was still in his twenties, Lippmann co-founded *The New Republic* with Herbert Croly and Walter Weyl. He went on to become a serious political philosopher as well as a newspaper columnist, winning the attention (if not always the agreement) of national political leaders from the era of Woodrow Wilson through that of Lyndon B. Johnson. In the history of American political writing, no figure has surpassed Lippmann in combining a scholar's detachment with a newspaperman's immersion in the issues and debates of the day. Long before the term "public intellectual" came into wide currency, Lippmann devoted himself to writing about strenuous topics for a large general audience—and to serving the public good.

Liberty and the News is not, today, among the best-known of Lippmann's books, and the slighting is unfortunate. Here, in three extended essays, Lippmann registered his disillusionment with the political and diplomatic results of the First World War, chiefly as a result of the propagandistic misinformation fed by the press to the public. Other commentators analyzed the problem in the simple economic and political terms made familiar by muckraking critics like Ida Tarbell and Upton Sinclair: the newspapers, supposedly, blindly served the interests of their right-wing big-business owners. Lippmann, however, developed a subtler line of reasoning, implicating the readers themselves in the press's deformation and citing numerous pressures, not all of them economic or political, that distorted the news. Above all, Lippmann perceived the crisis of the press as a political one that called into question the viability of democratic government in a large and complex society. Lippmann's proposed solution, although derided by some as elitist, helped to establish standards of objective factual reporting that became the norm at the most respected newspapers and other news-gathering institutions for decades to come.

The James Madison Library in American Politics will include the work of many political journalists, and it seems appropriate for Lippmann to head the list. It also seems appropriate to reissue the book in which he confronted most directly his own profession—elucidating his complaints but expressing his abiding hope that the public could yet receive the kind of accurate information on which any working democracy relies.

It is all the more urgent that Lippmann's criticisms be reconsidered today. Lippmann wrote of a very different press corps in a much simpler era. The proliferation of information sources after the advent of the Internet and cable television; the rise of the frenzied round-the-clock news cycle; the consequent decline in the subscription base for newspapers; the elimination, during the 1980s, of the Fairness Doctrine, which in one form or another had governed the public airwaves since the 1920s—all have profoundly altered journalism of every variety, especially political journalism. A rash of scandals over offenses ranging from plagiarism to new, insidious forms of government propagandizing has caused crises of confidence in newsrooms all across the country. But these current developments have simply enlarged what Lippmann identified long ago as "the pseudo-environment of reports, rumors, and guesses" that comes between people and the truth. His basic criticisms and analysis of that pseudo-environment are as pertinent as ever.

In his new foreword, Ronald Steel, the distinguished historian and author of an outstanding biography of Lippmann, places *Liberty and the News* in the context of Lippmann's career and highlights the gap between harsh reality and what Lippmann would later call "the original dogma of democracy." Sidney Blumenthal, the veteran journalist who also served in the Clinton White House, picks up in his afterword on Lippmann's concerns and indicts the reporting of political news during the George W. Bush presidency as a betrayal of Lippmann's ideal of objectivity. Both essays show that, whatever one's personal political beliefs may be, the existence of the press as a check on official power, the so-called Fourth Estate of American democracy, is by no means secure. Vulnerable to many forces, from inside as well as outside their profession, American reporters, editors, and publishers must constantly assess how well they are meeting their basic responsibilities to inform a democratic citizenry. Indeed, it appears that now as much as in 1920, and maybe more, the press needs to learn what those basic responsibilities are. *Liberty and the News* is a good place to start.

Sean Wilentz

Foreword
Ronald Steel

Beneath the deceptively bland title of this short book lie explosive ideas. They throw a disturbing light on the role of the press, the molding of public opinion, and the challenges to enlightened government in an age of mass democracy. Written in 1919 in the wake of a self-destructive war that spread ruin and revolution, this book reflects the disillusion, mixed with the lingering hope, of a young man who saw his ideals crushed, and yet sought a way by which his faith in popular government could be redeemed.

When the United States entered the European war in 1917 the twenty-seven-year-old Lippmann was a prominent editorialist at the influential journal of Progressive opinion, *The New Republic*. He had thrilled to Woodrow Wilson's pledge to "make the world safe for democracy" and was eager to do his part in that noble effort. He had become a journalist, rather than a businessman or professor, because he believed that nothing was more important than to help build a just and enlightened democratic society.

As a policy analyst in the government, he had worked on the team that formulated the Fourteen Points—Wilson's plan for an equitable postwar settlement among the warring European states.

Because of his skills as a writer he was also recruited to draft propaganda material to aid the Allied war effort by weakening German morale. That experience was a brief one, but it made an indelible impression upon him. It was to transform his whole attitude toward the role of the press in a free society.

Lippmann had eagerly supported the high ideals under which he believed the war was fought. But the aftermath brought for him, as for so many others, alarm and disillusion. The atavistic passions unleashed by the conflict, the vindictive peace treaty imposed by the victors upon the defeated, and the severe political repression that swept the United States during the postwar "Red Scare," forced him to question much of what he had taken for granted.

This did not lead him to retreat from the public arena and become part of the "lost generation" of cynics and exiles. But it did force him to reexamine his assumptions about the ability of the press under modern conditions to perform its role of providing for the public what he called its "bible of democracy."

The horrors of World War I had shattered his optimism about human nature. His propaganda work, reinforced by the repressive activities of the government's propaganda bureau, the Committee on Public Information, had made him realize how easily public opinion could be molded.

He had always believed that a free press was the cornerstone of democracy. He still believed that, but with a new qualification. In this seminal study, written shortly after his return from the war, he probed beyond the reaffirming conventional wisdom.

What if, he asked in these pages, the press—or the media, as we would now say—is not formally censored by church or state, and yet conveys news warped by bias, timidity, ignorance, or commercial pressure? Are people truly free if the information on which they base their judgments and elect their rulers is only haphazardly related to reality? Can popular government survive, he asks, when what he tellingly describes as the "manufacture of consent" is a private enterprise held to no standards of responsibility?

These are the probing questions that Lippmann addresses in this slim but disturbing volume. *Liberty and the News* reflects both the idealism of its young author and the skepticism about the traditional nostrums of press freedom and democracy engendered by the war. First published in 1920, it remains strikingly contemporary and relevant.

In these three essays we see Lippmann the journalist trying to come to grips with his realization that the press can be "free," yet often present a distorted image of the reality it reports. These concerns were soon to be developed into even more troubling conclusions in his landmark study, *Public Opinion,* and the deeply pessimistic *The Phantom Public.*

The issues that Lippmann raises here—the unsteady relationship between facts and news, the impact of distortion and propaganda on the judgments formed by the public, the assumption that the average person has the unbiased information needed to be a responsible citizen—go to the heart of a democratic theory based on popular consent.

In these pages Lippmann first posed the problem that remains unresolved, and is even more pressing today: how can a people, bombarded by information, assaulted by conflicting "facts," easily susceptible to rumor, distortion, and deliberate lies, make the informed judgments on which democracy depends?

Lippmann's work promoting the war had shown him how easily public opinion could be manipulated. But the aftermath of the war made him fully realize how dangerous this could be. The postwar anti-Bolshevik hysteria, resulting in the mass arrest of people charged with being subversives or "communists," the deportation of aliens, and widespread government censorship and repression, had instituted what a troubled Lippmann in 1920 described as a "reign of terror" fed by a "hurricane of demagoguery."

Although the Red Scare ultimately burned itself out, its scars remained. For Lippmann, its lessons were sobering. His writing took on a more skeptical tone. His studies had taught him that the "will of the people" is the sacred fount of democratic government. But now he was driven to consider a disquieting problem.

What if that will is deliberately manipulated by propaganda, or twisted by unscrupulous journalists or politicians? In that case the "will of the people" may rest on a shaky moral foundation. The problem was to find a way by which the rivers of opinion that fed public opinion could be purified. Only then could democratic government be fully responsible.

Traditional theories of government had become outmoded, according to Lippmann, because they failed to take into account two profound changes. The first was the concentration of power in the executive over the legislative branch. This was caused by the incessant growth of government in war and peace. The second was the increasingly important role of the press in molding public opinion. The impact of these two developments, he maintains in a striking observation that seems ever more relevant, changes the very balance of government.

The growth of executive power means that "decisions in the modern state" are no longer made as a result of the interaction of the legislature and the executive, of Congress and the White House, but rather "of public opinion and . . . executive [power]." The legislature can obstruct, but through the press the executive branch can go directly to the people.

At first glance this would seem to enhance the beneficial role of public opinion. But in effect what does the public really know? In large part it knows that which it learns from the press. This exalts the role of the press. But it also intensifies the need for accurate, unbiased reporting. For a democratic system to have real meaning, the news must be kept free of manipulation and pollution. Otherwise the "will of the people" becomes stripped of moral meaning. Truly democratic government becomes a fiction. For this reason, Lippmann insists, no task is more urgent than that of the protection of opinion. This had become the "basic problem of democracy."

Liberty had to be seen in a new light, one not defined by what is forbidden or permitted. Rather, liberty should be viewed as a process, "the name we give to measures by which we protect and increase the veracity of the information upon which we act." Liberty is not the absence of restraint, but "the construction of a system of information increasingly independent of opinion."

In this formulation the remedy lies not in providing greater tolerance for diverse opinions, but rather in protecting the stream of news from which opinions are formed. This means making publishers more accountable for the accuracy of the information they purvey, and making journalism a disciplined profession subject to rigorous standards of objectivity and professionalism.

This is a striking reformulation of the role of the press. But Lippmann takes his argument even further. It is no longer enough to say—as had thinkers of an earlier age like John Milton and John Stuart Mill—that the press must be free from censorship and intimidation, or that the news be protected from pollution by public officials and powerful interest groups. That is only the surface of the problem. Bias can be exposed and corrected. Journalists can be better trained and held to more rigorous standards. Intimidation by powerful commercial or government interests can be fought.

But what if the problem goes deeper than cronyism or corruption or government secrecy and manipulation? What if it goes beyond press freedom? In other words, what if the problem is not mechanical but organic? What if it is rooted not in what the press does, but in how people process the information they receive? What if it were lodged in human perception, in the very mind of the public itself?

In this short book, Lippmann suggests, but does not pursue, that disturbing thought. Yet tucked into this calm analysis of the role of public opinion in the modern state, of the importance of protecting the sources of information, and of the warnings against the "manufacture of consent" by both public and private manipulators, lies an explosive concept of a different order. It is slipped in tentatively, because Lippmann at this point had not himself probed its full implications. That would happen in the two books—*Public Opinion* and *The Phantom Public*—that follow this one in rapid fire succession. But a warning shot had been fired across the bow.

Lippmann's conceptual breakthrough—the analysis that makes *Liberty and the News* and its two successors so stimulating and also so intellectually unsettling—is that he makes the reader (and viewer in today's world) part of the equation. But he does not stop there. If the press is fallible, so is the reader. Because of his early interest in the newly developed theories of psychology, along with his experience in news manipulation, he could no longer believe that the problem could be resolved merely by greater tolerance for conflicting views, or more press resistance to social and government pressures.

The deeper problem, he came to realize, was located in the very nature of human perception. This is because we human beings do not automatically and objectively see what is before our eyes. We filter the outer world to correspond to our inner world. We interpret the world as we are trained to see it. This is the only way we can make sense of a cascade of images, impressions, and emotional triggers. "The world about which each man is supposed to have opinions has become so complicated as to defy his powers of understanding," he writes in these essays.

Most news comes secondhand rather than through direct observation. People respond to what they are told or what they infer. They are engulfed by opinions rather than truths, subjected to what Lippmann pointedly labels the "pseudo-environment of reports, rumors, and guesses." In an environment of fervent association and propaganda, "they believe whatever fits most comfortably with their prepossessions."

Here Lippmann paused. He had with great perception delineated the issue. But at this point he was still searching for a way to believe that the failures of the press could be remedied by more responsible reporting, that the average citizen could make intelligent judgments if presented with the facts.

Yet that faith was being undermined by his mounting skepticism. This skepticism, induced by his wartime experience, was deepened by recent studies in psychology and persuasion. The problem, he realized, went far beyond censorship, ignorance, or distortion. It went to the very working of the human mind. This soon forced him to confront a fact, as he stated the following year in *Public Opinion*—that the "pictures inside people's heads do not automatically correspond with the world outside."[1]

The implications of this were enormous. They led him to question what he called the "original dogma of democracy: that the knowledge needed for the management of human affairs comes up spontaneously from the human heart."[2] This meant that the average citizen, through no deliberate act of his own, might be only a flawed interpreter of the common interests. It also meant that the defects of democracy could not be cured merely by better reporting.

In these pages Lippmann was not yet ready to go so far. He wanted to find a way to bring the public's understanding of critical issues into line with objective reality. He believed that the press could help perform this role if it freed itself from special interest groups, commercial and governmental. He had seen the harm caused by deliberate or ignorant distortion of the news, and he still believed that by higher standards and more scrupulous training journalists could perform this vital public role. A truly democratic society, he believed, depended on that.

But his own harsh analysis had taken him to a critical juncture. The bitter experience of a terri-

[1] From chapter 1 of *Public Opinion*. See my *Walter Lippmann and the American Century* (Boston: Little, Brown, 1980), p. 181.

[2] From chapter 15 of *Public Opinion*. See *Walter Lippmann and the American Century*, p. 181.

ble war, entered under the banner of high ideals, but conducted under a shroud of lies and propaganda, lay just behind him. The shadow of disillusionment inherent in his own powerful argument had not yet overtaken him. In this important and unduly neglected book these two forces wage their preliminary battle.

Liberty and the News

In writing this tract I have dared to believe that many things were possible because of the personal example offered to all who practice journalism by Mr. C. P. Scott, for over forty-five years editor-in-chief of the *Manchester Guardian*. In the light of his career it cannot seem absurd or remote to think of freedom and truth in relation to the news.

Two of the essays in this volume, "What Modern Liberty Means" and "Liberty and the News," were published originally in the *Atlantic Monthly*. I wish to thank Mr. Ellery Sedgwick for the encouragement he gave me while writing them, and for permission to reprint them in this volume.

W. L.
New York City
January 1, 1920

1.

Journalism and the Higher Law

Volume I, Number I, of the first American news-paper was published in Boston on September 25, 1690. It was called *Publick Occurrences*. The second issue did not appear because the Governor and Council suppressed it. They found that Benjamin Harris, the editor, had printed "reflections of a very high nature."[1] Even today some of his reflections seem very high indeed. In his prospectus he had written:

> That something may be done toward the Curing, or at least the Charming of that Spirit of Lying, which prevails amongst us, wherefore nothing shall be entered, but what we have reason to believe is true, repairing to the best fountains for our Information. And when there appears any material mistake in anything that is collected, it shall be corrected in the next. Moreover, the Publisher of these Occurrences is willing to engage, that whereas, there are many False Reports, maliciously made, and spread

[1] "History of American Journalism," James Melvin Lee, Houghton Mifflin Co., 1917, p. 10.

among us, if any well-minded person will be at the pains to trace any such false Report, so far as to find out and Convict the First Raiser of it, he will in this Paper (unless just Advice be given to the contrary) expose the Name of such Person, as A malicious Raiser of a false Report. It is suppos'd that none will dislike this Proposal, but such as intend to be guilty of so villainous a Crime.

Everywhere today men are conscious that somehow they must deal with questions more intricate than any that church or school had prepared them to understand. Increasingly they know that they cannot understand them if the facts are not quickly and steadily available. Increasingly they are baffled because the facts are not available; and they are wondering whether government by consent can survive in a time when the manufacture of consent is an unregulated private enterprise. For in an exact sense the present crisis of western democracy is a crisis in journalism.

I do not agree with those who think that the sole cause is corruption. There is plenty of corruption, to be sure, moneyed control, caste pressure, financial and social bribery, ribbons, dinner parties, clubs, petty politics. The speculators in Russian rubles who lied on the Paris Bourse about the capture of Petrograd are not the only example of their species. And yet corruption does not explain the condition of modern journalism.

Mr. Franklin P. Adams wrote recently: "Now there is much pettiness—and almost incredible stupidity and ignorance—in the so-called free press; but it is the pettiness, etc., common to the so-called human race—a pettiness found in musicians, steamfitters, landlords, poets, and waiters. And when Miss Lowell [who had made the usual aristocratic complaint] speaks of the incurable desire in all American newspapers to make fun of everything in season and out, we quarrel again. There is an incurable desire in American newspapers to take things much more seriously than they deserve. Does Miss Lowell read the ponderous news from Washington? Does she read the society news? Does she, we wonder, read the newspapers?"

Mr. Adams does read them, and when he writes that the newspapers take things much more seriously than they deserve, he has, as the mayor's wife remarked to the queen, said a mouthful. Since the war, especially, editors have come to believe that their highest duty is not to report but to instruct, not to print news but to save civilization, not to publish what Benjamin Harris calls "the Circumstances of Publique Affairs, both abroad and at home," but to keep the nation on the straight and narrow path. Like the Kings of England, they have elected themselves Defenders of the Faith. "For five years," says Mr. Cobb of the

New York World, "there has been no free play of public opinion in the world. Confronted by the inexorable necessities of war, governments conscripted public opinion. . . . They goose-stepped it. They taught it to stand at attention and salute. . . . It sometimes seems that after the armistice was signed, millions of Americans must have taken a vow that they would never again do any thinking for themselves. They were willing to die for their country, but not willing to think for it." That minority, which is proudly prepared to think for it, and not only prepared, but cocksure that it alone knows how to think for it, has adopted the theory that the public should know what is good for it.

The work of reporters has thus become confused with the work of preachers, revivalists, prophets and agitators. The current theory of American newspaperdom is that an abstraction like the truth and a grace like fairness must be sacrificed whenever anyone thinks the necessities of civilization require the sacrifice. To Archbishop Whately's dictum that it matters greatly whether you put truth in the first place or the second, the candid expounder of modern journalism would reply that he put truth second to what he conceived to be the national interest. Judged simply by their product, men like Mr. Ochs or Viscount Northcliffe believe that their respective nations will perish and civilization decay unless their idea of what is patriotic is permitted to temper the curiosity of their readers.

They believe that edification is more important than veracity. They believe it profoundly, violently, relentlessly. They preen themselves upon it. To patriotism, as they define it from day to day, all other considerations must yield. That is their pride. And yet what is this but one more among myriad examples of the doctrine that the end justifies the means. A more insidiously misleading rule of conduct was, I believe, never devised among men. It was a plausible rule as long as men believed that an omniscient and benevolent Providence taught them what end to seek. But now that men are critically aware of how their purposes are special to their age, their locality, their interests, and their limited knowledge, it is blazing arrogance to sacrifice hard-won standards of credibility to some special purpose. It is nothing but the doctrine that I want what I want when I want it. Its monuments are the Inquisition and the invasion of Belgium. It is the reason given for almost every act of unreason, the law invoked whenever lawlessness justifies itself. At bottom it is nothing but the anarchical nature of man imperiously hacking its way through.

Just as the most poisonous form of disorder is the mob incited from high places, the most immoral act the immorality of a government, so the most destructive form of untruth is sophistry and propaganda by those whose profession it is to report the news. The news columns are common carriers. When those who control them arrogate to themselves the right to determine by their own consciences what shall be reported and for what purpose, democracy is unworkable. Public opinion is blockaded. For when a people can no longer confidently repair 'to the best fountains for their information,' then anyone's guess and anyone's rumor, each man's hope and each man's whim becomes the basis of government. All that the sharpest critics of democracy have alleged is true, if there is no steady supply of trustworthy and relevant news. Incompetence and aimlessness, corruption and disloyalty, panic and ultimate disaster, must come to any people which is denied an assured access to the facts. No one can manage anything on pap. Neither can a people.

Statesmen may devise policies; they will end in futility, as so many have recently ended, if the propagandists and censors can put a painted screen where there should be a window to the world. Few episodes in recent history are more poignant than that of the British Prime Minister, sitting at the breakfast table with that morning's paper before him protesting that he cannot do the sensible thing in regard to Russia because a powerful newspaper proprietor has drugged the public. That incident is a photograph of the supreme danger which confronts popular government. All other dangers are contingent upon it, for the news is the chief source of the opinion by which government now proceeds. So long as there is interposed between the ordinary citizen and the facts a news organization determining by entirely private and unexamined standards, no matter how lofty, what he shall know, and hence what he shall believe, no one will be able to say that the substance of democratic government is secure. The theory of our constitution, says Mr. Justice Holmes, is that truth is the only ground upon which men's wishes safely can be carried out.[2] In so far as those who purvey the news make of their own beliefs a higher law than truth, they are attacking the foundations of our constitutional system. There can be no higher law in journalism than to tell the truth and shame the devil.

That I have few illusions as to the difficulty of truthful reporting anyone can see who reads these pages. If truthfulness were simply a matter of sincerity the future would be rather simple. But the modern news problem is not solely a question of the newspaperman's morals. It is, as I have tried to show in what follows, the intricate result of a civilization too extensive for any man's personal observation. As the problem is manifold, so must be the remedy. There is no panacea. But however puzzling the matter may be, there are some things that anyone may assert about it, and assert with-

[2] Supreme Court of the United States, No. 316, October term, 1919, *Jacob Abrams et al., Plaintiffs in Error vs. the United States.*

out fear of contradiction. They are that there *is* a problem of the news which is of absolutely basic importance to the survival of popular government, and that the importance of that problem is not vividly realized nor sufficiently considered.

In a few generations it will seem ludicrous to historians that a people professing government by the will of the people should have made no serious effort to guarantee the news without which a governing opinion cannot exist. "Is it possible," they will ask, "that at the beginning of the Twentieth Century nations calling themselves democracies were content to act on what happened to drift across their doorsteps; that apart from a few sporadic exposures and outcries they made no plans to bring these common carriers under social control; that they provided no genuine training schools for the men upon whose sagacity they were dependent; above all that their political scientists went on year after year writing and lecturing about government without producing one, one single, significant study of the process of public opinion?" And then they will recall the centuries in which the Church enjoyed immunity from criticism, and perhaps they will insist that the news structure of secular society was not seriously examined for analogous reasons.

When they search into the personal records they will find that among journalists, as among the clergy, institutionalism had induced the usual prudence. I have made no criticism in this book which is not the shoptalk of reporters and editors. But only rarely do newspapermen take the general public into their confidence. They will have to sooner or later. It is not enough for them to struggle against great odds, as many of them are doing, wearing out their souls to do a particular assignment well. The philosophy of the work itself needs to be discussed; the news about the news needs to be told. For the news about the government of the news structure touches the center of all modern government.

They need not be much concerned if leathery-minded individuals ask What is Truth of all who plead for the effort of truth in modern journalism. Jesting Pilate asked the same question, and he also would not stay for an answer. No doubt an organon of news reporting must wait upon the development of psychology and political science. But resistance to the inertias of the profession, heresy to the institution, and the willingness to be fired rather than write what you do not believe, these wait on nothing but personal courage. And without the assistance which they will bring from within the profession itself, democracy through it will deal with the problem somehow, will deal with it badly.

The essays which follow are an attempt to describe the character of the problem, and to indicate headings under which it may be found useful to look for remedies.

2.

What Modern Liberty Means

From our recent experience it is clear that the traditional liberties of speech and opinion rest on no solid foundation. At a time when the world needs above all other things the activity of generous imaginations and the creative leadership of planning and inventive minds, our thinking is shriveled with panic. Time and energy that should go to building and restoring are instead consumed in warding off the pin-pricks of prejudice and fighting a guerilla war against misunderstanding and intolerance. For suppression is felt, not simply by the scattered individuals who are actually suppressed. It reaches back into the steadiest minds, creating tension everywhere; and the tension of fear produces sterility. Men cease to say what they think; and when they cease to say it, they soon cease to think it. They think in reference to their critics and not in reference to the facts. For when thought becomes socially hazardous, men spend more time wondering about the hazard than they do in cultivating their thought. Yet nothing is more certain than that mere bold resistance will not permanently liberate men's minds. The problem is not only greater than that, but different, and the time is ripe for reconsideration. We have learned that many of the hard-won rights of man are utterly insecure. It may be that we cannot make them secure simply by imitating the earlier champions of liberty.

Something important about the human character was exposed by Plato when, with the spectacle of Socrates's death before him, he founded Utopia on a censorship stricter than any which exists on this heavily censored planet. His intolerance seems strange. But it is really the logical expression of an impulse that most of us have not the candor to recognize. It was the service of Plato to formulate the dispositions of men in the shape of ideals, and the surest things we can learn from him are not what we ought to do, but what we are inclined to do. We are peculiarly inclined to suppress whatever impugns the security of that to which we have given our allegiance. If our loyalty is turned to what exists, intolerance begins at its frontiers; if it is turned, as Plato's was, to Utopia, we shall find Utopia defended with intolerance.

There are, so far as I can discover, no absolutists of liberty; I can recall no doctrine of liberty, which, under the acid test, does not become contingent upon some other ideal. The goal is never liberty, but liberty for something or other. For liberty is a condition under which activity takes place, and men's interests attach themselves primarily to their activities and what is necessary to fulfill them, not to the abstract requirements of any activity that might be conceived.

And yet controversialists rarely take this into account. The battle is fought with banners on which are inscribed absolute and universal ideals. They are not absolute and universal in fact. No man has ever thought out an absolute or a universal ideal in politics, for the simple reason that nobody knows enough, or can know enough, to do it. But we all use absolutes, because an ideal which seems to exist apart from time, space, and circumstance has a prestige that no candid avowal of special purpose can ever have. Looked at from one point of view universals are part of the fighting apparatus in men. What they desire enormously they easily come to call God's will, or their nation's purpose. Looked at genetically, these idealizations are probably born in that spiritual reverie where all men live most of the time. In reverie there is neither time, space, nor particular reference, and hope is omnipotent. This omnipotence, which is denied to them in action, nevertheless illuminates activity with a sense of utter and irresistible value.

The classic doctrine of liberty consists of absolutes. It consists of them except at the critical points where the author has come into contact with objective difficulties. Then he introduces into the argument, somewhat furtively, a reservation which liquidates its universal meaning and reduces the exalted plea for liberty in general to a special argument for the success of a special purpose.

There are at the present time, for instance, no more fervent champions of liberty than the western sympathizers with the Russian Soviet government. Why is it that they are indignant when Mr. Burleson suppresses a newspaper and complacent when Lenin does? And, *vice versa*, why is it that the anti-Bolshevist forces in the world are in favor of restricting constitutional liberty as a preliminary to establishing genuine liberty in Russia? Clearly the argument about liberty has little actual relation to the existence of it. It is the purpose of the social conflict, not the freedom of opinion, that lies close to the heart of the partisans. The word liberty is a weapon and an advertisement, but certainly not an ideal which transcends all special aims.

If there were any man who believed in liberty apart from particular purposes, that man would be a hermit contemplating all existence with a hopeful and neutral eye. For him, in the last analysis, there could be nothing worth resisting, nothing particularly worth attaining, nothing particularly worth defending, not even the right of hermits to contemplate existence with a cold and neutral eye. He would be loyal simply to the possibilities of the human spirit, even to those possibilities which most seriously impair its variety and its health. No such man has yet counted much in the history of politics. For what every theorist of liberty has meant is that certain types of behavior and classes of opinion hitherto regulated should be somewhat differently regulated in the future. What each seems to say is that opinion and action should be free; that liberty is the highest and most sacred interest of life. But somewhere each of them inserts a weasel clause to the effect that "of course" the freedom granted shall not be employed too destructively. It is this clause which checks exuberance and reminds us that, in spite of appearances, we are listening to finite men pleading a special cause.

Among the English classics none are more representative than Milton's *Areopagitica* and the essay *On Liberty* by John Stuart Mill. Of living men Mr. Bertrand Russell is perhaps the most outstanding advocate of liberty. The three together are a formidable set of witnesses. Yet nothing is easier than to draw texts from each which can be cited either as an argument for absolute liberty or as an excuse for as much repression as seems desirable at the moment. Says Milton:

> Yet if all cannot be of one mind, as who looks they should be? this doubtles is more wholsome, more prudent, and more Christian that many be tolerated, rather than all compell'd.

So much for the generalization. Now for the qualification which follows immediately upon it.

I mean not tolerated Popery, and open super-
stition, which as it extirpats all religions and
civill supremacies, so itself should be extir-
pat, provided first that all charitable and
compassionat means be used to win and re-
gain the weak and misled: that also which is
impious or evil absolutely either against faith
or maners no law can possibly permit, that
intends not to unlaw it self: but those neighboring differences, or rather *indifferences,*
are what I speak of, whether in some point of
doctrine or of discipline, which though they
may be many, yet need not interrupt the unity
of spirit, if we could but find among us the
bond of peace.

With this as a text one could set up an inquisition. Yet it occurs in the noblest plea for liberty
that exists in the English language. The critical
point in Milton's thought is revealed by the word
"indifferences." The area of opinion which he
wished to free comprised the "neighboring differences" of certain Protestant sects, and only these
where they were truly ineffective in manners and
morals. Milton, in short, had come to the conclusion that certain conflicts of doctrine were sufficiently insignificant to be tolerated. The conclusion depended far less upon his notion of the
value of liberty than upon his conception of God
and human nature and the England of his time.

He urged indifference to things that were becoming indifferent.

If we substitute the word indifference for the word liberty, we shall come much closer to the real intention that lies behind the classic argument. Liberty is to be permitted where differences are of no great moment. It is this definition which has generally guided practice. In times when men feel themselves secure, heresy is cultivated as the spice of life. During a war liberty disappears as the community feels itself menaced. When revolution seems to be contagious, heresy-hunting is a respectable occupation. In other words, when men are not afraid, they are not afraid of ideas; when they are much afraid, they are afraid of anything that seems, or can even be made to appear, seditious. That is why nine-tenths of the effort to live and let live consists in proving that the thing we wish to have tolerated is really a matter of indifference.

In Mill this truth reveals itself still more clearly. Though his argument is surer and completer than Milton's, the qualification is also surer and completer.

Such being the reasons which make it imperative that human beings should be free to form opinions, and to express their opinions without reserve; and such the baneful consequences to the intellectual and through that to the moral nature of man, unless this liberty is either conceded or asserted in spite of prohibition, let us next examine whether the same reasons do not require that men should be free to act upon their opinions, to carry these out in their lives, without hindrance, either moral or physical, from their fellow men, so long as it is at their own risk and peril. *This last proviso is of course indispensable.* No one pretends that actions should be as free as opinions. On the contrary, *even opinions lose their immunity* when the circumstances in which they are expressed are such as to constitute their expression a positive instigation to some mischievous act.

"At their own risk and peril." In other words, at the risk of eternal damnation. The premise from which Mill argued was that many opinions then under the ban of society were of no interest to society, and ought therefore not to be interfered with. The orthodoxy with which he was at war was chiefly theocratic. It assumed that a man's opinions on cosmic affairs might endanger his personal salvation and make him a dangerous member of society. Mill did not believe in the theological view, did not fear damnation, and was convinced that morality did not depend upon the religious sanction. In fact, he was convinced that a more reasoned morality could be formed by laying aside theological assumptions. "But no one pretends that actions should be as free as opinions." The plain truth is that Mill did not believe that much action would result from the toleration of those opinions in which he was most interested.

Political heresy occupied the fringe of his attention, and he uttered only the most casual comments. So incidental are they, so little do they impinge on his mind, that the arguments of this staunch apostle of liberty can be used honestly, and in fact are used, to justify the bulk of the suppressions which have recently occurred. "Even opinions lose their immunity, *when the circumstances* in which they are expressed are such as to constitute their expression a positive instigation to some mischievous act." Clearly there is no escape here for Debs or Haywood or obstructors of Liberty Loans. The argument used is exactly the one employed in sustaining the conviction of Debs.

In corroboration Mill's single concrete instance may be cited: "An opinion that corn dealers are starvers of the poor, or that private property is robbery, ought to be unmolested when simply circulated through the press, but may justly incur punishment when delivered orally to an excited mob assembled before the house of a corn dealer, or when handed about among the same mob in the form of a placard."

Clearly Mill's theory of liberty wore a different complexion when he considered opinions which might directly affect social order. Where the stimulus of opinion upon action was effective he could say with entire complacency, "The liberty of the individual must be thus far limited; he must not make himself a nuisance to other people." Because Mill believed this, it is entirely just to infer that the distinction drawn between a speech or placard and publication in the press would soon have broken down for Mill had he lived at a time when the press really circulated and the art of type-display had made a newspaper strangely like a placard.

On first acquaintance no man would seem to go further than Mr. Bertrand Russell in loyalty to what he calls "the unfettered development of all the instincts that build up life and fill it with mental delights." He calls these instincts "creative"; and against them he sets off the "possessive impulses." These, he says, should be restricted by "a public authority, a repository of practically irresistible force whose function should be primarily to repress the private use of force." Where Milton said no "tolerated Popery," Mr. Russell says, no tolerated "possessive impulses." Surely he is open to the criticism that, like every authoritarian who has preceded him, he is interested in the unfettered development of only that which seems good to him. Those who think that "enlightened selfishness" produces social harmony will tolerate more of the possessive impulses, and will be inclined to put certain of Mr. Russell's creative impulses under lock and key.

The moral is, not that Milton, Mill, and Bertrand Russell are inconsistent, or that liberty is to be obtained by arguing for it without qualifications. The impulse to what we call liberty is as strong in these three men as it is ever likely to be in our society. The moral is of another kind. It is that the traditional core of liberty, namely, the notion of indifference, is too feeble and unreal a doctrine to protect the purpose of liberty, which is the furnishing of a healthy environment in which human judgment and inquiry can most successfully organize human life. Too feeble, because in time of stress nothing is easier than to insist, and by insistence to convince, that tolerated indifference is no longer tolerable because it has ceased to be indifferent.

It is clear that in a society where public opinion has become decisive, nothing that counts in the formation of it can really be a matter of indifference. When I say "can be," I am speaking literally. What men believed about the constitution of heaven became a matter of indifference when heaven disappeared in metaphysics; but what they believe about property, government, conscription, taxation, the origins of the late war, or the origins of the Franco-Prussian War, or the distribution of Latin culture in the vicinity of copper mines, constitutes the difference between life and death, prosperity and misfortune, and it will never on this earth be tolerated as indifferent, or not interfered with, no matter how many noble arguments are made for liberty, or how many martyrs give their lives for it. If widespread tolerance of opposing views is to be achieved in modern society, it will not be simply by fighting the Debs' cases through the courts, and certainly not by threatening to upset those courts if they do not yield to the agitation. The task is fundamentally of another order, requiring other methods and other theories.

The world about which each man is supposed to have opinions has become so complicated as to defy his powers of understanding. What he knows of events that matter enormously to him, the purposes of governments, the aspirations of peoples, the struggle of classes, he knows at second, third, or fourth hand. He cannot go and see for himself. Even the things that are near to him have become too involved for his judgment. I know of no man, even among those who devote all of their time to watching public affairs, who can even pretend to keep track, at the same time, of his city government, his state government, Congress, the departments, the industrial situation, and the rest of the world. What men who make the study of politics a vocation cannot do, the man who has an hour a day for newspapers and talk cannot possibly hope to do. He must seize catchwords and headlines or nothing.

This vast elaboration of the subject-matter of politics is the root of the whole problem. News comes from a distance; it comes helter-skelter, in inconceivable confusion; it deals with matters that are not easily understood; it arrives and is assimilated by busy and tired people who must take what is given to them. Any lawyer with a sense of evidence knows how unreliable such information must necessarily be.

The taking of testimony in a trial is hedged about with a thousand precautions derived from long experience of the fallibility of the witness and the prejudices of the jury. We call this, and rightly, a fundamental phase of human liberty. But in public affairs the stake is infinitely greater. It involves the lives of millions, and the fortune of everybody. The jury is the whole community, not even the qualified voters alone. The jury is everybody who creates public sentiment—chattering gossips, unscrupulous liars, congenital liars, feeble-minded people, prostitute minds, corrupting agents. To this jury any testimony is submitted, is submitted in any form, by any anonymous person, with no test of reliability, no test of credibility, and no penalty for perjury. If I lie in a lawsuit involving the fate of my neighbor's cow, I can go to jail. But if I lie to a million readers in a matter involving war and peace, I can lie my head off, and, if I choose the right series of lies, be entirely irresponsible. Nobody will punish me if I lie about Japan, for example. I can announce that every Japanese valet is a reservist, and every Japanese art store a mobilization center. I am immune. And if there should be hostilities with Japan, the more I lied the more popular I should be. If I asserted that the Japanese secretly drank the blood of children, that Japanese women were unchaste, that the Japanese were really not a branch of the human race after all, I guarantee that most of the newspapers would print it eagerly, and that I could get a hearing in churches all over the country. And all this for the simple reason that the public, when it is dependent on testimony and protected by no rules of evidence, can act only on the excitement of its pugnacities and its hopes.

The mechanism of the news-supply has developed without plan, and there is no one point in it at which one can fix the responsibility for truth. The fact is that the subdivision of labor is now accompanied by the subdivision of the news-organization. At one end of it is the eye-witness, at the other, the reader. Between the two is a vast, expensive transmitting and editing apparatus. This machine works marvelously well at times, particularly in the rapidity with which it can report the score of a game or a transatlantic flight, or the death of a monarch, or the result of an election. But where the issue is complex, as for example in the matter of the success of a policy, or the social conditions among a foreign people—that is to say, where the real answer is neither yes or no, but subtle, and a matter of balanced evidence—the subdivision of the labor involved in the report causes no end of derangement, misunderstanding, and even misrepresentation.

Thus the number of eye-witnesses capable of honest statement is inadequate and accidental. Yet the reporter making up his news is dependent upon the eye-witnesses. They may be actors in the event. Then they can hardly be expected to have perspective. Who, for example, if he put aside his own likes and dislikes would trust a Bolshevik's account of what exists in Soviet Russia or an ex-iled Russian prince's story of what exists in Siberia? Sitting just across the frontier, say in Stockholm, how is a reporter to write dependable news when his witnesses consist of *emigrés* or Bolshevist agents?

At the Peace Conference, news was given out by the agents of the conferees and the rest leaked through those who were clamoring at the doors of the Conference. Now the reporter, if he is to earn his living, must nurse his personal contacts with the eye-witnesses and privileged informants. If he is openly hostile to those in authority, he will cease to be a reporter unless there is an opposition party in the inner circle who can feed him news. Failing that, he will know precious little of what is going on.

Most people seem to believe that, when they meet a war correspondent or a special writer from the Peace Conference, they have seen a man who has seen the things he wrote about. Far from it. Nobody, for example, saw this war. Neither the men in the trenches nor the commanding general. The men saw their trenches, their billets, sometimes they saw an enemy trench, but nobody, unless it be the aviators, saw a battle. What the correspondents saw, occasionally, was the terrain over which a battle had been fought; but what they reported day by day was what they were told at press headquarters, and of that only what they were allowed to tell.

At the Peace Conference the reporters were allowed to meet periodically the four least important members of the Commission, men who themselves had considerable difficulty in keeping track of things, as any reporter who was present will testify. This was supplemented by spasmodic personal interviews with the commissioners, their secretaries, their secretaries' secretaries, other newspaper men, and confidential representatives of the President, who stood between him and the impertinences of curiosity. This and the French press, than which there is nothing more censored and inspired, a local English trade-journal of the expatriates, the gossip of the Crillon lobby, the Majestic, and the other official hotels, constituted the source of the news upon which American editors and the American people have had to base one of the most difficult judgments of their history. I should perhaps add that there were a few correspondents occupying privileged positions with foreign governments. They wore ribbons in their button-holes to prove it. They were in many ways the most useful correspondents because they always revealed to the trained reader just what it was that their governments wished America to believe.

The news accumulated by the reporter from his witnesses has to be selected, if for no other reason than that the cable facilities are limited. At the cable office several varieties of censorship intervene. The legal censorship in Europe is political as well as military, and both words are elastic. It has been applied, not only to the substance of the news, but to the mode of presentation, and even to the character of the type and the position on the page. But the real censorship on the wires is the cost of transmission. This in itself is enough to limit any expensive competition or any significant independence. The big Continental news agencies are subsidized. Censorship operates also through congestion and the resultant need of a system of priority. Congestion makes possible good and bad service, and undesirable messages are not infrequently served badly.

When the report does reach the editor, another series of interventions occurs. The editor is a man who may know all about something, but he can hardly be expected to know all about everything. Yet he has to decide the question which is of more importance than any other in the formation of opinions, the question where attention is to be directed. In a newspaper the heads are the foci of attention, the odd corners the fringe; and whether one aspect of the news or another appears in the center or at the periphery makes all the difference in the world. The news of the day as it reaches the newspaper office is an incredible medley of fact, propaganda, rumor, suspicion, clues, hopes, and fears, and the task of selecting and ordering that news is one of the truly sacred and priestly offices in a democracy. For the newspaper is in all literalness the bible of democracy, the book out of which a people determines its conduct. It is the only serious book most people read. It is the only book they read every day. Now the power to determine each day what shall seem important and what shall be neglected is a power unlike any that has been exercised since the Pope lost his hold on the secular mind.

The ordering is not done by one man, but by a host of men, who are on the whole curiously unanimous in their selection and in their emphasis. Once you know the party and social affiliations of a newspaper, you can predict with considerable certainty the perspective in which the news will be displayed. This perspective is by no means altogether deliberate. Though the editor is ever so much more sophisticated than all but a minority of his readers, his own sense of relative importance is determined by rather standardized constellations of ideas. He very soon comes to believe that his habitual emphasis is the only possible one.

Why the editor is possessed by a particular set of ideas is a difficult question in social psychology, of which no adequate analysis has been made. But we shall not be far wrong if we say that he deals with the news in reference to the prevailing *mores* of his social group. These *mores* are of course in a large measure the product of what previous newspapers have said; and experience shows that, in order to break out of this circle, it has been necessary at various times to create new forms of journalism, such as the national monthly, the critical weekly, the circular, the paid advertisements of ideas, in order to change the emphasis which had become obsolete and habit-ridden.

Into this extremely refractory, and I think increasingly disserviceable mechanism, there has been thrown, especially since the outbreak of war, another monkey-wrench—propaganda. The word, of course, covers a multitude of sins and a few virtues. The virtues can be easily separated out, and given another name, either advertisement or advocacy. Thus, if the National Council of Belgravia wishes to publish a magazine out of its own funds, under its own imprint, advocating the annexation of Thrums, no one will object. But if, in support of that advocacy, it gives to the press stories that are lies about the atrocities committed in Thrums; or, worse still, if those stories seem to come from Geneva, or Amsterdam, not from the press-service of the National Council of Belgravia, then Belgravia is conducting propaganda. If, after arousing a certain amount of interest in itself, Belgravia then invites a carefully selected correspondent, or perhaps a labor leader, to its capital, puts him up at the best hotel, rides him around in limousines, fawns on him at banquets, lunches with him very confidentially, and then puts him through a conducted tour so that he shall see just what will create the desired impression, then again Belgravia is conducting propaganda. Or if Belgravia happens to possess the greatest trombone-player in the world, and if she sends him over to charm the wives of influential husbands, Belgravia is, in a less objectionable way, perhaps, committing propaganda, and making fools of the husbands.

Now, the plain fact is that out of the troubled areas of the world the public receives practically nothing that is not propaganda. Lenin and his enemies control all the news there is of Russia, and no court of law would accept any of the testimony as valid in a suit to determine the possession of a donkey. I am writing many months after the Armistice. The Senate is at this moment engaged in debating the question whether it will guarantee the frontiers of Poland; but what we learn of Poland we learn from the Polish Government and the Jewish Committee. Judgment on the vexed issues of Europe is simply out of the question for the average American; and the more cocksure he is, the more certainly is he the victim of some propaganda.

These instances are drawn from foreign affairs, but the difficulty at home, although less flagrant, is nevertheless real. Theodore Roosevelt, and Leonard Wood after him, have told us to think nationally. It is not easy. It is easy to parrot what those people say who live in a few big cities and who have constituted themselves the only true and authentic voice of America. But beyond that it is difficult. I live in New York and I have not the vaguest idea what Brooklyn is interested in. It is possible, with effort, much more effort than most people can afford to give, for me to know what a few organized bodies like the Non-Partisan League, the National Security League, the American Federation of Labor, and the Republican National Committee are up to; but what the unorganized workers, and the unorganized farmers, the shopkeepers, the local bankers and boards of trade are thinking and feeling, no one has any means of knowing, except perhaps in a vague way at election time. To think nationally means, at least, to take into account the major interests and needs and desires of this continental population; and for that each man would need a staff of secretaries, traveling agents, and a very expensive press-clipping bureau.

We do not think nationally because the facts that count are not systematically reported and presented in a form we can digest. Our most abysmal ignorance occurs where we deal with the immigrant. If we read his press at all, it is to discover "Bolshevism" in it and to blacken all immigrants with suspicion. For his culture and his aspirations, for his high gifts of hope and variety, we have neither eyes nor ears. The immigrant colonies are like holes in the road which we never notice until we trip over them. Then, because we have no current information and no background of facts, we are, of course, the undiscriminating objects of any agitator who chooses to rant against "foreigners."

Now, men who have lost their grip upon the relevant facts of their environment are the inevitable victims of agitation and propaganda. The quack, the charlatan, the jingo, and the terrorist, can flourish only where the audience is deprived of independent access to information. But where all news comes at second-hand, where all the testimony is uncertain, men cease to respond to truths, and respond simply to opinions. The environment in which they act is not the realities themselves, but the pseudo-environment of reports, rumors, and guesses. The whole reference of thought comes to be what somebody asserts, not what actually is. Men ask, not whether such and such a thing occurred in Russia, but whether Mr. Raymond Robins is at heart more friendly to the Bolsheviki than Mr. Jerome Landfield. And so, since they are deprived of any trustworthy means of knowing what is really going on, since everything is on the plane of assertion and propaganda, they believe whatever fits most comfortably with their prepossessions.

That this breakdown of the means of public knowledge should occur at a time of immense change is a compounding of the difficulty. From bewilderment to panic is a short step, as everyone knows who has watched a crowd when danger threatens. At the present time a nation easily acts like a crowd. Under the influence of headlines and panicky print, the contagion of unreason can easily spread through a settled community. For when the comparatively recent and unstable nervous organization which makes us capable of responding to reality as it is, and not as we should wish it, is baffled over a continuing period of time, the more primitive but much stronger instincts are let loose.

War and Revolution, both of them founded on censorship and propaganda, are the supreme destroyers of realistic thinking, because the excess of danger and the fearful overstimulation of passion unsettle disciplined behavior. Both breed fanatics of all kinds, men who, in the words of Mr. Santayana, have redoubled their effort when they have forgotten their aim. The effort itself has become the aim. Men live in their effort, and for a time find great exaltation. They seek stimulation of their effort rather than direction of it. That is why both in war and revolution there seems to operate a kind of Gresham's Law of the emotions, in which leadership passes by a swift degradation from a Mirabeau to a Robespierre; and in war, from a high-minded statesmanship to the depths of virulent, hating jingoism.

The cardinal fact always is the loss of contact with objective information. Public as well as private reason depends upon it. Not what somebody says, not what somebody wishes were true, but what is so beyond all our opining, constitutes the touchstone of our sanity. And a society which lives at second-hand will commit incredible follies and countenance inconceivable brutalities if that contact is intermittent and untrustworthy. Demagoguery is a parasite that flourishes where discrimination fails, and only those who are at grips with things themselves are impervious to it. For, in the last analysis, the demagogue, whether of the Right or the Left, is, consciously or unconsciously an undetected liar.

Many students of politics have concluded that,

because public opinion was unstable, the remedy lay in making government as independent of it as possible. The theorists of representative government have argued persistently from this premise against the believers in direct legislation. But it appears now that, while they have been making their case against direct legislation, rather successfully it seems to me, they have failed sufficiently to notice the increasing malady of representative government.

Parliamentary action is becoming notoriously ineffective. In America certainly the concentration of power in the Executive is out of all proportion either to the intentions of the Fathers or to the orthodox theory of representative government. The cause is fairly clear. Congress is an assemblage of men selected for local reasons from districts. It brings to Washington a more or less accurate sense of the superficial desires of its constituency. In Washington it is supposed to think nationally and internationally. But for that task its equipment and its sources of information are hardly better than that of any other reader of the newspaper. Except for its spasmodic investigating committees, Congress has no particular way of informing itself. But the Executive has. The Executive is an elaborate hierarchy reaching to every part of the nation and to all parts of the world. It has an independent machinery, fallible and not too truthworthy, of course, but nevertheless a machinery of intelligence. It can be informed and it can act, whereas Congress is not informed and cannot act.

Now the popular theory of representative government is that the representatives have the information and therefore create the policy which the executive administers. The more subtle theory is that the executive initiates the policy which the legislature corrects in accordance with popular wisdom. But when the legislature is haphazardly informed, this amounts to very little, and the people themselves prefer to trust the executive which knows, rather than the Congress which is vainly trying to know. The result has been the development of a kind of government which has been harshly described as plébiscite autocracy, or government by newspapers. Decisions in the modern state tend to be made by the interaction, not of Congress and the executive, but of public opinion and the executive.

Public opinion for this purpose finds itself collected about special groups which act as extra-legal organs of government. There is a labor nucleus, a farmers' nucleus, a prohibition nucleus, a National Security League nucleus, and so on. These groups conduct a continual electioneering campaign upon the unformed, exploitable mass of public opinion. Being special groups, they have special sources of information, and what they lack in the way of information is often manufactured. These conflicting pressures beat upon the executive departments and upon Congress, and formulate the conduct of the government. The government itself acts in reference to these groups far more than in reference to the district congressmen. So politics as it is now played consists in coercing and seducing the representative by the threat and the appeal of these unofficial groups. Sometimes they are the allies, sometimes the enemies, of the party in power, but more and more they are the energy of public affairs. Government tends to operate by the impact of controlled opinion upon administration. This shift in the locus of sovereignty has placed a premium upon the manufacture of what is usually called consent. No wonder that the most powerful newspaper proprietor in the English-speaking world declined a mere government post.

No wonder, too, that the protection of the sources of its opinion is the basic problem of democracy. Everything else depends upon it. Without protection against propaganda, without standards of evidence, without criteria of emphasis, the living substance of all popular decision is exposed to every prejudice and to infinite exploitation. That is why I have argued that the older doctrine of liberty was misleading. It did not assume a public opinion that governs. Essentially it demanded toleration of opinions that were, as Milton said, indifferent. It can guide us little in a world where opinion is sensitive and decisive.

The axis of the controversy needs to be shifted. The attempt to draw fine distinctions between "liberty" and "license" is no doubt part of the day's work, but it is fundamentally a negative part. It consists in trying to make opinion responsible to prevailing social standards, whereas the really important thing is to try and make opinion increasingly responsible to the facts. There can be no liberty for a community which lacks the information by which to detect lies. Trite as the conclusion may at first seem, it has, I believe, immense practical consequences, and may perhaps offer an escape from the logomachy into which the contests of liberty so easily degenerate.

It may be bad to suppress a particular opinion, but the really deadly thing is to suppress the news. In time of great insecurity, certain opinions acting on unstable minds may cause infinite disaster. Knowing that such opinions necessarily originate in slender evidence, that they are propelled more by prejudice from the rear than by reference to realities, it seems to me that to build the case for liberty upon the dogma of their unlimited prerogatives is to build it upon the poorest foundation. For, even though we grant that the world is best served by the liberty of all opinion, the plain fact is that men are too busy and too much concerned to fight more than spasmodically for such liberty.

When freedom of opinion is revealed as freedom of error, illusion, and misinterpretation, it is virtually impossible to stir up much interest in its behalf. It is the thinnest of all abstractions and an over-refinement of mere intellectualism. But people, wide circles of people, are aroused when their curiosity is baulked. The desire to know, the dislike of being deceived and made game of, is a really powerful motive, and it is that motive that can best be enlisted in the cause of freedom.

What, for example, was the one most general criticism of the work of the Peace Conference? It was that the covenants were not openly arrived at. This fact stirred Republican Senators, British Labor, the whole gamut of parties from the Right to the Left. And in the last analysis lack of information about the Conference *was* the origin of its difficulties. Because of the secrecy endless suspicion was aroused; because of it the world seemed to be presented with a series of accomplished facts which it could not reject and did not wish altogether to accept. It was lack of information which kept public opinion from affecting the negotiations at the time when intervention would have counted most and cost least. Publicity occurred when the covenants were arrived at, with all the emphasis on the *at*. This is what the Senate objected to, and this is what alienated much more liberal opinion than the Senate represents.

In a passage quoted previously in this essay,

Milton said that differences of opinion, "which though they may be many, yet need not interrupt the unity of spirit, if we could but find among us the bond of peace." There is but one kind of unity possible in a world as diverse as ours. It is unity of method, rather than of aim; the unity of the disciplined experiment. There is but one bond of peace that is both permanent and enriching: the increasing knowledge of the world in which experiment occurs. With a common intellectual method and a common area of valid fact, differences may become a form of co-operation and cease to be an irreconcilable antagonism.

That, I think, constitutes the meaning of freedom for us. We cannot successfully define liberty, or accomplish it, by a series of permissions and prohibitions. For that is to ignore the content of opinion in favor of its form. Above all, it is an attempt to define liberty of opinion in terms of opinion. It is a circular and sterile logic. A useful definition of liberty is obtainable only by seeking the principle of liberty in the main business of human life, that is to say, in the process by which men educate their response and learn to control their environment. In this view liberty is the name we give to measures by which we protect and increase the veracity of the information upon which we act.

3.

Liberty and the News

The debates about liberty have hitherto all been attempts to determine just when in the series from Right to Left the censorship should intervene. In the preceding paper I ventured to ask whether these attempts do not turn on a misconception of the problem. The conclusion reached was that, in dealing with liberty of opinion, we were dealing with a subsidiary phase of the whole matter; that, so long as we were content to argue about the privileges and immunities of opinion, we were missing the point and trying to make bricks without straw. We should never succeed even in fixing a standard of tolerance for opinions, if we concentrated all our attention on the opinions. For they are derived, not necessarily by reason, to be sure, but somehow, from the stream of news that reaches the public, and the protection of that stream is the critical interest in a modern state. In going behind opinion to the information which it exploits, and in making the validity of the news our ideal, we shall be fighting the battle where it is really being fought. We shall be protecting for the public interest that which all the special interests in the world are most anxious to corrupt.

As the sources of the news are protected, as the information they furnish becomes accessible and usable, as our capacity to read that information is educated, the old problem of tolerance will wear a new aspect. Many questions which seem hopelessly insoluble now will cease to seem important enough to be worth solving. Thus the advocates of a larger freedom always argue that true opinions will prevail over error; their opponents always claim that you can fool most of the people most of the time. Both statements are true, but both are half-truths. True opinions can prevail only if the facts to which they refer are known; if they are not known, false ideas are just as effective as true ones, if not a little more effective.

The sensible procedure in matters affecting the liberty of opinion would be to ensure as impartial an investigation of the facts as is humanly possible. But it is just this investigation that is denied us. It is denied us, because we are dependent upon the testimony of anonymous and untrained and prejudiced witnesses; because the complexity of the relevant facts is beyond the scope of our hurried understanding; and finally, because the process we call education fails so lamentably to educate the sense of evidence or the power of penetrating to the controlling center of a situation. The task of liberty, therefore, falls roughly under three heads, protection of the sources of the news, organization of the news so as to make it comprehensible, and education of human response.

We need, first, to know what can be done with the existing news-structure, in order to correct its grosser evils. How far is it useful to go in fixing personal responsibility for the truthfulness of news? Much further, I am inclined to think, than we have ever gone. We ought to know the names of the whole staff of every periodical. While it is not necessary, or even desirable, that each article should be signed, each article should be documented, and false documentation should be illegal. An item of news should always state whether it is received from one of the great news-agencies, or from a reporter, or from a press bureau. Particular emphasis should be put on marking news supplied by press bureaus, whether they are labeled "Geneva," or "Stockholm," or "El Paso."

One wonders next whether anything can be devised to meet that great evil of the press, the lie which, once under way, can never be tracked down. The more scrupulous papers will, of course, print a retraction when they have unintentionally injured someone; but the retraction rarely compensates the victim. The law of libel is a clumsy and expensive instrument, and rather useless to private individuals or weak organizations because of the gentlemen's agreement which obtains in the newspaper world. After all, the remedy for libel is not money damages, but an undoing of the injury. Would it be possible then to establish courts of honor in which publishers should be compelled to meet their accusers and, if found guilty of misrepresentation, ordered to publish the correction in the particular form and with the prominence specified by the finding of the court? I do not know. Such courts might prove to be a great nuisance, consuming time and energy and attention, and offering too free a field for individuals with a persecution mania.

Perhaps a procedure could be devised which would eliminate most of these inconveniences. Certainly it would be a great gain if the accountability of publishers could be increased. They exercise more power over the individual than is healthy, as everybody knows who has watched the yellow press snooping at keyholes and invading the privacy of helpless men and women. Even more important than this, is the utterly reckless power of the press in dealing with news vitally affecting the friendship of peoples. In a Court of Honor, possible perhaps only in Utopia, voluntary associations working for decent relations with other peoples might hale the jingo and the subtle propagandist before a tribunal, to prove the reasonable truth of his assertion or endure the humiliation of publishing prominently a finding against his character.

This whole subject is immensely difficult, and full of traps. It would be well worth an intensive investigation by a group of publishers, lawyers, and students of public affairs. Because in some form or other the next generation will attempt to bring the publishing business under greater social control. There is everywhere an increasingly angry disillusionment about the press, a growing sense of being baffled and misled; and wise publishers will not pooh-pooh these omens. They might well note the history of prohibition, where a failure to work out a programme of temperance brought about an undiscriminating taboo. The regulation of the publishing business is a subtle and elusive matter, and only by an early and sympathetic effort to deal with great evils can the more sensible minds retain their control. If publishers and authors themselves do not face the facts and attempt to deal with them, some day Congress, in a fit of temper, egged on by an outraged public opinion, will operate on the press with an ax. For somehow the community must find a way of making the men who publish news accept responsibility for an honest effort not to misrepresent the facts.

But the phrase "honest effort" does not take us very far. The problem here is not different from that which we begin dimly to apprehend in the field of government and business administration. The untrained amateur may mean well, but he knows not how to do well. Why should he? What are the qualifications for being a surgeon? A certain minimum of special training. What are the qualifications for operating daily on the brain and heart of a nation? None. Go some time and listen to the average run of questions asked in interviews with Cabinet officers—or anywhere else.

I remember one reporter who was detailed to the Peace Conference by a leading news-agency. He came around every day for "news." It was a time when Central Europe seemed to be disintegrating, and great doubt existed as to whether governments would be found with which to sign a peace. But all that this "reporter" wanted to know was whether the German fleet, then safely interned at Scapa Flow, was going to be sunk in the North Sea. He insisted every day on knowing that. For him it was the German fleet or nothing. Finally, he could endure it no longer. So he anticipated Admiral Reuther and announced, in a dispatch to his home papers, that the fleet would be sunk. And when I say that a million American adults learned all that they ever learned about the Peace Conference through this reporter, I am stating a very moderate figure.

He suggests the delicate question raised by the schools of journalism: how far can we go in turning newspaper enterprise from a haphazard trade into a disciplined profession? Quite far, I imagine, for it is altogether unthinkable that a society like ours should remain forever dependent upon untrained accidental witnesses. It is no answer to say that there have been in the past, and that there are now, first-rate correspondents. Of course there are. Men like Brailsford, Oulahan, Gibbs, Lawrence, Swope, Strunsky, Draper, Hard, Dillon, Lowry, Levine, Ackerman, Ray Stannard Baker, Frank Cobb, and William Allen White, know their way about in this world. But they are eminences on a rather flat plateau. The run of the news is handled by men of much smaller caliber. It is handled by such men because reporting is not a dignified profession for which men will invest the time and cost of an education, but an underpaid, insecure, anonymous form of drudgery, conducted on catch-as-catch-can principles. Merely to talk about the reporter in terms of his real importance to civilization will make newspaper men laugh. Yet reporting is a post of peculiar honor. Observation must precede every other activity, and the public observer (that is, the reporter) is a man of critical value. No amount of money or effort spent in fitting the right men for this work could possibly be wasted, for the health of society depends upon the quality of the information it receives.

Do our schools of journalism, the few we have, make this kind of training their object, or are they trade-schools designed to fit men for higher salaries in the existing structure? I do not presume to answer the question, nor is the answer of great moment when we remember how small a part these schools now play in actual journalism. But it is important to know whether it would be worth while to endow large numbers of schools on the model of those now existing, and make their diplomas a necessary condition for the practice of reporting. It is worth considering. Against the idea lies the fact that it is difficult to decide just what reporting is—where in the whole mass of printed matter it begins and ends. No one would wish to set up a closed guild of reporters and thus exclude invaluable casual reporting and writing. If there is anything in the idea at all, it would apply only to the routine service of the news through large organizations.

Personally I should distrust too much ingenuity of this kind, on the ground that, while it might correct certain evils, the general tendency would be to turn the control of the news over to unenterprising stereotyped minds soaked in the traditions of a journalism always ten years out of date. The better course is to avoid the deceptive short cuts, and make up our minds to send out into reporting a generation of men who will by sheer superiority, drive the incompetents out of business. That means two things. It means a public recognition of the dignity of such a career, so that it will cease to be the refuge of the vaguely talented. With this increase of prestige must go a professional training in journalism in which the ideal of objective testimony is cardinal. The cynicism of the trade needs to be abandoned, for the true patterns of the journalistic apprentice are not the slick persons who scoop the news, but the patient and fearless men of science who have labored to see what the world really is. It does not matter that the news is not susceptible of mathematical statement. In fact, just because news is complex and slippery, good reporting requires the exercise of the highest of the scientific virtues. They are the habits of ascribing no more credibility to a statement than it warrants, a nice sense of the probabilities, and a keen understanding of the quantitative importance of particular facts. You can judge the general reliability of any observer most easily by the estimate he puts upon the reliability of his own report. If you have no facts of your own with which to check him, the best rough measurement is to wait and see whether he is aware of any limitations in himself; whether he knows that he saw only part of the event he describes; and whether he has any background of knowledge against which he can set what he thinks he has seen.

This kind of sophistication is, of course, necessary for the merest pretense to any education. But for different professions it needs to be specialized in particular ways. A sound legal training is pervaded by it, but the skepticism is pointed to the type of case with which the lawyer deals. The reporter's work is not carried on under the same conditions, and therefore requires a different specialization. How he is to acquire it is, of course, a pedagogical problem requiring an inductive study of the types of witness and the sources of information with whom the reporter is in contact.

Some time in the future, when men have thoroughly grasped the role of public opinion in society, scholars will not hesitate to write treatises on evidence for the use of news-gathering services. No such treatise exists today, because political science has suffered from that curious prejudice of the scholar which consists in regarding an irrational phenomenon as not quite worthy of serious study.

Closely akin to an education in the tests of credibility is rigorous discipline in the use of words. It is almost impossible to overestimate the confusion in daily life caused by sheer inability to use language with intention. We talk scornfully of "mere words." Yet through words the whole vast process of human communication takes place. The sights and sounds and meanings of nearly all that we deal with as "politics," we learn, not by our own experience, but through the words of others. If those words are meaningless lumps charged with emotion, instead of the messengers of fact, all sense of evidence breaks down. Just so long as big words like Bolshevism, Americanism, patriotism, pro-Germanism, are used by reporters to cover anything and anybody that the biggest fool at large wishes to include, just so long shall we be seeking our course through a fog so dense that we cannot tell whether we fly upside-down or right-side-up. It is a measure of our education as a people that so many of us are perfectly content to live our political lives in this fraudulent environment of unanalyzed words. For the reporter, abracadabra is fatal. So long as he deals in it, he is gullibility itself, seeing nothing of the world, and living, as it were, in a hall of crazy mirrors.

Only the discipline of a modernized logic can open the door to reality. An overwhelming part of the dispute about "freedom of opinion" turns on words which mean different things to the censor and the agitator. So long as the meanings of the words are not dissociated, the dispute will remain a circular wrangle. Education that shall make men masters of their vocabulary is one of the central interests of liberty. For such an education alone can transform the dispute into debate from similar premises.

A sense of evidence and a power to define words must for the modern reporter be accompanied by a working knowledge of the main stratifications and currents of interest. Unless he knows that "news" of society almost always starts from a special group, he is doomed to report the surface of events. He will report the ripples of a passing steamer, and forget the tides and the currents and the ground-swell. He will report what Kolchak or Lenin says, and see what they do only when it confirms what he thinks they said. He will deal with the flicker of events and not with their motive. There are ways of reading that flicker so as to discern the motive, but they have not been formulated in the light of recent knowledge. Here is big work for the student of politics. The good reporter reads events with an intuition trained by wide personal experience. The poor reporter cannot read them, because he is not even aware that there is anything in particular to read.

And then the reporter needs a general sense of what the world is doing. Emphatically he ought not to be serving a cause, no matter how good. In his professional activity it is no business of his to care whose ox is gored. To be sure, when so much reporting is *ex parte,* and hostile to insurgent forces, the insurgents in self-defense send out *ex parte* reporters of their own. But a community cannot rest content to learn the truth about the Democrats by reading the Republican papers, and the truth about the Republicans by reading the Democratic papers. There is room, and there is need, for disinterested reporting; and if this sounds like a counsel of perfection now, it is only because the science of public opinion is still at the point where astronomy was when theological interests proclaimed the conclusions that all research must vindicate.

While the reporter will serve no cause, he will possess a steady sense that the chief purpose of "news" is to enable mankind to live successfully toward the future. He will know that the world is a process, not by any means always onward and upward, but never quite the same. As the observer of the signs of change, his value to society depends upon the prophetic discrimination with which he selects those signs.

But the news from which he must pick and choose has long since become too complicated even for the most highly trained reporter. The work, say, of the government is really a small part of the day's news, yet even the wealthiest and most resourceful newspapers fail in their efforts to report "Washington." The high lights and the disputes and sensational incidents are noted, but no one can keep himself informed about his Congressman or about the individual departments, by reading the daily press. This failure in no way reflects on the newspapers. It results from the intricacy and unwieldiness of the subject-matter. Thus, it is easier to report Congress than it is to report the departments, because the work of Congress crystallizes crudely every so often in a rollcall. But administration, although it has become more important than legislation, is hard to follow, because its results are spread over a longer period of time, and its effects are felt in ways that no reporter can really measure.

Theoretically Congress is competent to act as the critical eye on administration. Actually, the investigations of Congress are almost always plan-less raids, conducted by men too busy and too lit-tle informed to do more than catch the grosser evils, or intrude upon good work that is not un-derstood. It was a recognition of these difficulties that was the cause of two very interesting experi-ments in late years. One was the establishment of more or less semi-official institutes of government research; the other, the growth of specialized pri-vate agencies which attempt to give technical summaries of the work of various branches of the government. Neither experiment has created much commotion: yet together they illustrate an idea which, properly developed, will be increas-ingly valuable to an enlightened public opinion.

Their principle is simple. They are expert orga-nized reporters. Having no horror of dullness, no interest in being dramatic, they can study statis-tics and orders and reports which are beyond the digestive powers of a newspaper man or of his readers. The lines of their growth would seem to be threefold: to make a current record, to make a running analysis of it, and on the basis of both, to suggest plans.

Record and analysis require an experimental formulation of standards by which the work of government can be tested. Such standards are not to be evolved off-hand out of anyone's conscious-ness. Some have already been worked out exper-imentally, others still need to be discovered; all need to be refined and brought into perspective by the wisdom of experience. Carried out competently, the public would gradually learn to substitute objective criteria for gossip and intuitions. One can imagine a public-health service subjected to such expert criticism. The institute of research publishes the death-rate as a whole for a period of years. It seems that for a particular season the rate is bad in certain maladies, that in others the rate of improvement is not sufficiently rapid. These facts are compared with the expenditures of the service, and with the main lines of its activity. Are the bad results due to the causes beyond the control of the service? Do they indicate a lack of foresight in asking appropriations for special work? Or in the absence of novel phenomena, do they point to a decline of the personnel, or in its morale? If the latter, further analysis may reveal that salaries are too low to attract men of ability, or that the head of the service by bad management has weakened the interest of his staff.

When the work of government is analyzed in some such way as this, the reporter deals with a body of knowledge that has been organized for his apprehension. In other words, he is able to report the "news," because between him and the raw material of government there has been interposed a more or less expert political intelligence. He ceases to be the ant, described by William

James, whose view of a building was obtained by crawling over the cracks in the walls.

These political observatories will, I think, be found useful in all branches of government, national, state, municipal, industrial, and even in foreign affairs. They should be clearly out of reach either of the wrath or of the favor of the office-holders. They must, of course, be endowed, but the endowment should be beyond the immediate control of the legislature and of the rich patron. Their independence can be partially protected by the terms of the trust; the rest must be defended by the ability of the institute to make itself so much the master of the facts as to be impregnably based on popular confidence.

One would like to think that the universities could be brought into such a scheme. Were they in close contact with the current record and analysis, there might well be a genuine "field work" in political science for the students; and there could be no better directing idea for their more advanced researches than the formulation of the intellectual methods by which the experience of government could be brought to usable control. After all, the purpose of studying "political science" is to be able to act more effectively in politics, the word effectively being understood in the largest and, therefore, the ideal sense. In the universities men should be able to think patiently and generously for the good of society. If they do not, surely one of the reasons is that thought terminates in doctor's theses and brown quarterlies, and not in the critical issues of politics.

On first thought, all this may seem rather a curious direction for an inquiry into the substance of liberty. Yet we have always known, as a matter of common sense, that there was an intimate connection between "liberty" and the use of liberty. Every one who has examined the subject at all has had to conclude that tolerance *per se* is an arbitrary line, and that, in practice, the determining factor is the significance of the opinion to be tolerated. This study is based on an avowal of that fact. Once it is avowed, there seems to be no way of evading the conclusion that liberty is not so much permission as it is the construction of a system of information increasingly independent of opinion. In the long run it looks as if opinion could be made at once free and enlightening only by transferring our interest from "opinion" to the objective realities from which it springs. This thought has led us to speculations on ways of protecting and organizing the stream of news as the source of all opinion that matters. Obviously these speculations do not pretend to offer a fully considered or a completed scheme. Their nature forbids it, and I should be guilty of the very opinionativeness I have condemned, did these essays claim to be anything more than tentative indications of the more important phases of the problem.

Yet I can well imagine their causing a considerable restlessness in the minds of some readers. Standards, institutes, university research, schools of journalism, they will argue, may be all right, but they are a gray business in a vivid world. They blunt the edge of life; they leave out of account the finely irresponsible opinion thrown out by the creative mind; they do not protect the indispensable novelty from philistinism and oppression. These proposals of yours, they will say, ignore the fact that such an apparatus of knowledge will in the main be controlled by the complacent and the traditional, and the execution will inevitably be illiberal.

There is force in the indictment. And yet I am convinced that we shall accomplish more by fighting for truth than by fighting for our theories. It is a better loyalty. It is a humbler one, but it is also more irresistible. Above all it is educative. For the real enemy is ignorance, from which all of us, conservative, liberal, and revolutionary, suffer. If our effort is concentrated on our desires—be it our desire to have and to hold what is good, our desire to remake peacefully, or our desire to transform suddenly—we shall divide hopelessly and irretrievably. We must go back of our opinions to the neutral facts for unity and refreshment of spirit. To deny this, it seems to me, is to claim that the mass of men is impervious to education, and to deny that, is to deny the postulate of democracy, and to seek salvation in a dictatorship. There is, I am convinced, nothing but misery and confusion that way. But I am equally convinced that democracy will degenerate into this dictatorship either of the Right or of the Left, if it does not become genuinely self-governing. That means, in terms of public opinion, a resumption of that contact between beliefs and realities which we have been losing steadily since the small-town democracy was absorbed into the Great Society.

The administration of public information toward greater accuracy and more successful analysis is the highway of liberty. It is, I believe, a matter of first-rate importance that we should fix this in our minds. Having done so, we may be able to deal more effectively with the traps and the lies and the special interests which obstruct the road and drive us astray. Without a clear conception of what the means of liberty are, the struggle for free speech and free opinion easily degenerates into a mere contest of opinion.

But realization is not the last step, though it is the first. We need be under no illusion that the stream of news can be purified simply by pointing out the value of purity. The existing news-structure may be made serviceable to democracy along the general lines suggested, by the training of the journalist, and by the development of expert record and analysis. But while it may be, it will not be, simply by saying that it ought to be. Those who are now in control have too much at stake, and they control the source of reform itself.

Change will come only by the drastic competition of those whose interests are not represented in the existing news-organization. It will come only if organized labor and militant liberalism set a pace which cannot be ignored. Our sanity and, therefore, our safety depend upon this competition, upon fearless and relentless exposure conducted by self-conscious groups that are now in a minority. It is for these groups to understand that the satisfaction of advertising a pet theory is as nothing compared to the publication of the news. And having realized it, it is for them to combine their resources and their talent for the development of an authentic news-service which is invincible because it supplies what the community is begging for and cannot get.

All the gallant little sheets expressing particular programmes are at bottom vanity, and in the end, futility, so long as the reporting of daily news is left in untrained and biased hands. If we are to move ahead, we must see a great independent journalism, setting standards for commercial journalism, like those which the splendid English coöperative societies are setting for commercial business. An enormous amount of money is dribbled away in one fashion or another on little papers, mass-meetings, and what not. If only some considerable portion of it could be set aside to establish a central international news-agency, we should make progress. We cannot fight the untruth which envelops us by parading our opinions. We can do it only by reporting the facts, and we do not deserve to win if the facts are against us.

The country is spotted with benevolent foundations of one kind or another, many of them doing nothing but pay the upkeep of fine buildings and sinecures. Organized labor spends large sums of money on politics and strikes which fail because it is impossible to secure a genuine hearing in public opinion. Could there be a pooling of money for a news-agency? Not, I imagine, if its object were to further a cause. But suppose the plan were for a news-service in which editorial matter was rigorously excluded, and the work was done by men who had already won the confidence of the public by their independence? Then, perhaps.

At any rate, our salvation lies in two things: ultimately, in the infusion of the news-structure by men with a new training and outlook; immediately, in the concentration of the independent forces against the complacency and bad service of the routineers. We shall advance when we have learned humility; when we have learned to seek the truth, to reveal it and publish it; when we care more for that than for the privilege of arguing about ideas in a fog of uncertainty.

Afterword
Sidney Blumenthal

From the moment he entered onto the public scene as a writer for the new journal of opinion, *The New Republic*, established in 1914, Walter Lippmann's precocity was apparent. He made his way almost effortlessly into the highest levels of society and politics, his uninterrupted elevation almost proof in itself of the progressive view of history. Yet his thinking, particularly about the craft of journalism, derived chiefly from experience with the curdling of American Progressivism and the end of its innocence after World War I.

Lippmann sharpened his early disillusionment into a perfectly pitched tone of omniscience. He descended from his lofty peak as a wise man with an Olympian air of detachment, permitting mere mortals to benefit from his counsel. Oracle to the powers that be, he was also the father of modern objectivity. He never saw any contradiction between his deeds and words or felt any need to pause over any supposed conflict. Nor did any public figure suggest that there was anything untoward or unseemly in his alliances or aversions. Instead, they sought his approbation and cordiality. His immersion in politics while holding forth as a disinterested observer did not taint him as hypocritical or false. Everyone understood that he was Walter Lippmann. If there were a prevailing prejudice about him, it was a tendency to judge him by his cogency and influence.

The standards of objective journalism Lippmann painstakingly advocated in the early twentieth century, and which were adopted as ideal goals by major news organizations in midcentury, have long since been traduced, trampled, and trashed. The journalistic world before the Vietnam War was, to be sure, hardly a golden age. The pliability of much of the national press in the face of Senator Joseph McCarthy's red-baiting smear campaigns occurred in the middle of those happy days. Golden ages glitter only in retrospect as viewed from the junkyard of the present. Nonetheless, there has been a steady degeneration of the press over the past few decades, involving both the willful self-destruction of hard-won credibility and the rationalization of dull incomprehension as invulnerable self-importance. The gap between Lippmann's ideals and present realities is one of the major reasons why *Liberty and the News* remains so pertinent—and so troubling—nearly ninety years after its publication.

"For in an exact sense the present crisis of western democracy is a crisis of journalism," Lippmann wrote. That sentence was distilled from years of hope turned to despair. Lippmann had ferried from the offices of *The New Republic*, located in New York, to the White House, where he helped work on speeches for Woodrow Wilson. After the entry of the United States in the world war in 1917, Lippmann enthusiastically accepted an appointment as the U.S. representative on the Inter-Allied Propaganda Board, with the rank of captain. But Captain Lippmann soon crossed swords with George Creel, chief of the Committee on Public Information, an official federal government agency that whipped up war support through jingoism. When Lippmann submitted a blistering report in 1918 on how the committee manipulated news to foster national hysteria, Creel sought his dismissal—and Lippmann quit his post to assist the U.S. delegation at the Versailles peace conference. The year following the war, 1919, began with Wilson greeted as a messiah and ended with him politically broken and physically paralyzed. His collapse personified the wreckage of Progressive idealism. Lippmann focused his attention on the part played by the press.

"Everywhere today," Lippmann wrote in *Liberty and the News*, "men are conscious that somehow they must deal with questions more intricate than any that church or school had prepared them to understand. Increasingly they know that they cannot understand them if the facts are not quickly and steadily available. Increasingly they are baffled because the facts are not available; and they are wondering whether government by consent can survive in a time when the manufacture of consent is an unregulated private enterprise."

Lippmann had witnessed firsthand how the "manufacture of consent" had deranged democracy. But he did not hold those in government solely responsible. He also described how the press corps was carried away on the wave of patriotism and became self-censors, enforcers, and sheer propagandists. Their careerism, cynicism, and error made them destroyers of "liberty of opinion" and agents of intolerance, who subverted the American constitutional system of self-government. Even the great newspaper owners, he wrote, "believe that edification is more important than veracity. They believe it profoundly, violently, relentlessly. They preen themselves upon it. To patriotism, as they define it from day to day, all other considerations must yield. That is their pride. And yet what is this but one more among myriad examples of the doctrine that the end justifies the means? A more insidiously misleading rule of conduct was, I believe, never devised among men."

Public opinion was not a free marketplace of ideas, but was channeled and polluted by the managers of news. They concentrated their power at the expense of accurately informing the public, whose fears and hatreds they exploited. Reason was impossible to sustain in the whirlwind. Lippmann wrote:

Just as the most poisonous form of disorder is the mob incited from high places, the most immoral act the immorality of a government, so the most destructive form of untruth is sophistry and propaganda by those whose profession it is to report the news. The news columns are common carriers. When those who control them arrogate to themselves the right to determine by their own consciences what shall be reported and for what purpose, democracy is unworkable. Public opinion is blockaded. For when a people can no longer confidently repair "to the best foundations for their information," then anyone's guess and anyone's rumor, each man's hope and each man's whim becomes the basis of government. All that the sharpest critics of democracy have alleged is true, if there is no steady supply of trustworthy and relevant news. Incompetence and aimlessness, corruption and disloyalty, panic and ultimate disaster, must come to any people which is denied an assured access to the facts. No one can manage anything on pap. Neither can a people.

A year before *Liberty and the News* appeared, the famous muckraking journalist and novelist Upton Sinclair, author of *The Jungle*, published *The Brass Check*, the first contemporary exposé of the press as a corrupt special interest. Sinclair asserted that the press simply reflected its big-business ownership and did its bidding. Lippmann's analysis, though, was at once more subtle and more penetrating, elucidating a form of corruption that ran to the foundations of the nation's politics.

By substituting propaganda for truth, brandishing jingoism to enforce conformity, and asserting arrogance and certainty over skepticism and humility, Lippmann contended, the manufacturers of consent confounded democracy. "In so far as those who purvey the news make of their own beliefs a higher law than truth, they are attacking the foundations of our constitutional system. There can be no higher law in journalism than to tell the truth and shame the devil."

•••

Woodrow Wilson waged war to make the world "safe for democracy" and to establish an international order based on collective security. Nearly a century later, President George W. Bush appropriated Wilson's rhetoric as a gloss on preemptive war and unilateralism. Neoconservatism stood Wilsonianism on its head, and, had he lived to see the day, Lippmann might have rubbed his eyes like Rip Van Winkle at how much had changed. Yet Lippmann also would have discovered a depressingly familiar press corps on a bandwagon of jingoism, disseminating falsehoods leaked by government officials, engaging in ruthless self-censorship, and preening in careerist triumphalism.

The behavior of the press corps under Bush revealed a corruption more in line with Lippmann's analysis than Sinclair's, although Sinclair's stress on the primacy of vulgar economics had its play, too. Indeed, Bush administration officials, including Vice President Dick Cheney, complained to the chief executive officers of major media corporations about reports and reporters, and the pressure fell down the chain of command like an anvil. Nearly every correspondent, producer, and commentator on every broadcast and cable network outlet was keenly aware of such interventions and adjusted accordingly. The cable network MSNBC's dismissal in February 2003, one month before the invasion of Iraq, of the popular Phil Donahue as host of a public affairs program that had raised skeptical questions about the rationale for the war was cautionary and symptomatic. An internal memo claimed that Donahue presented "a difficult public face for NBC in a time of war" while "at the same time our competitors are waving the flag at every opportunity."[1] For crass reasons, jingoism became a criterion for presentation of news.

[1] Eric Boehlert, *Lapdogs: How the Press Rolled Over for Bush* (New York: Free Press, 2006), p. 213.

But economics did not explain everything. In 2002, the conservative Fox News anchor Brit Hume, well aware of the scent of fear in the air, declared ABC News unpatriotic: "Over at ABC News, where the wearing of American flag lapel pins is banned, Peter Jennings [the news anchor] and his team have devoted far more time to the coverage of civilian casualties in Afghanistan than either of their broadcast network competitors."[2]

Hume's attack reflected the general conservative argument that the press was a bastion of "liberal bias," and was thus untrustworthy and even potentially perfidious in the war on terror. A conservative columnist, Andrew Sullivan, who later became a disillusioned administration critic, articulated most clearly the right-wing dichotomy of domestic good-and-evil in the immediate aftermath of September 11. "The middle part of the country—the great red zone that voted for Bush—is clearly ready for war," he wrote. "The decadent Left in its enclaves on the coasts is not dead—and may well mount what amounts to a fifth column."[3]

In an atmosphere rife with intimidation, key reporters and editorial writers for major newspapers, including the *New York Times* and the

[2] Michael Scherer, "Framing the Flag," *Columbia Journalism Review*, March/April 2002.

[3] Andrew Sullivan, "America at War: America Wakes Up to a World of Fear," *Sunday Times of London*, September 16, 2001.

Washington Post, also became cheerleaders for the neoconservative project. In the case of the *Times*, the editors' avid desire for scoops initially overwhelmed all else—and put the newspaper in the forefront in publishing falsehoods, on its front page, about Iraq's supposed stockpiles of weapons of mass destruction. In May 2004, the *Times*, its false reports now exposed, issued an extraordinary "Editors' Note": "Information that was controversial then, and seems questionable now, was insufficiently qualified or allowed to stand unchallenged. Looking back, we wish we had been more aggressive in re-examining the claims as new evidence emerged—or failed to emerge." Thereafter, though, the *Times*' reckless search for scoops gave way to the suppression of news that might damage the Bush White House. For more than a year after its apology over its WMD coverage—and throughout the 2004 election campaign—the paper refused to publish its reporters' accounts of how the Bush administration was engaged in domestic spying by evading the legal court established by the Foreign Intelligence Surveillance Act.[4]

In the rush to war, from September 2002 through February 2003, the *Washington Post* editorialized in favor of an invasion twenty-six

---

[4] James Risen and Eric Lichtblau, "Bush Lets U.S. Spy on Callers Without Courts," *New York Times*, December 16, 2005.

times. Every single editorial contained disinformation, some of it directly leaked by administration officials. On February 6, 2003, the day after Secretary of State Colin Powell's speech to the United Nations Security Council presenting supposed evidence of WMD, the *Post* ran an editorial headline, "Irrefutable," and said "it is hard to imagine how anyone could doubt that Iraq possesses weapons of mass destruction." (Two years later, Powell described his speech, which had been revealed as a string of disinformation, as a "blot" on his record, "terrible," and "painful.") Afterward, the *Post*'s editorial board issued no "Editor's Note" or clarification like the one that had appeared in the *New York Times*. Factual reporting that suggested doubt about the existence of Saddam Hussein's weapons of mass destruction had been either buried or suppressed by the *Post*'s editors. And, with the notable exception of the Knight Ridder news service, the *Post*'s coverage was typical of the supposedly "liberal" press corps.[5]

In the heady days before, during, and long after

[5] See "Irrefutable," *Washington Post*, February 6, 2003; Howard Kurtz, "The Post on WMDs: An Inside Story: Prewar Articles Questioning Threat Often Didn't Make Front Page," *Washington Post*, August 12, 2004; James P. Pinkerton, "The Washington Post's Creeping Hawkishness," *Salon*, August 4, 2004, http://archive.salon.com/opinion/feature/2004/08/04/washington_post/index.html; Michael Massing, "Now They Tell Us," *New York Review of Books*, February 26, 2004.

the press embedded with military units invading Iraq, making them feel close to the action, Bush was presented as decisive, commanding, and knowledgeable; National Security Advisor Condoleezza Rice was brilliant; Vice President Cheney wise; Secretary of Defense Donald Rumsfeld savvy; and Karl Rove a genius. In the fall of 2002, as the administration ratcheted up its propaganda offensive before the Iraq war, Bob Woodward, the renowned investigative reporter of Watergate, published a book, *Bush At War*—based on leaks of select national security documents and interviews with officials up to and including President Bush. Senior officials, in fact, were ordered to grant Woodward his access. George Tenet, then the CIA director, later wrote in his memoir: "[W]e kept getting calls from the White House saying, 'We're cooperating fully with Woodward, and we would like CIA to do so, too.'"[6] Through administration packaging of high-level contacts and carefully chosen classified material, the imprimatur of the famous and trusted journalist was stamped on stereotypes favorable to the administration.

In early 2004, after receiving a call from the chairman of the Joint Chiefs of Staff, General Richard Myers, CBS News withheld its own re-

---

[6] George Tenet, *At the Center of the Storm: My Years at the CIA* (New York: HarperCollins, 2007), p. 365.

porting on torture at the Abu Ghraib prison in Baghdad. (The *New Yorker* broke the story even as CBS held it back.) In May of that year, Senator Mark Dayton, Democrat of Minnesota, questioned Secretary of Defense Rumsfeld and General Myers about the incident. The transcript of the Senate Armed Services Committee hearing reads:

DAYTON: Mr. Secretary, were you aware or did you authorize General Myers to call CBS to suppress their news report?

RUMSFELD: I don't have any idea if he discussed it with me. I was—I don't know. I don't think he did.

DAYTON: So over the last two weeks, calling CBS to suppress the news report. You don't—

RUMSFELD: ["]Suppress["] is not the right word at all.

DAYTON: I'm sorry, sir, but I—

RUMSFELD: And it's an inaccurate word, I should say.

DAYTON: General Myers, did you discuss it with the secretary?

MYERS: This had been worked at lower levels with the secretary's staff and my staff for some time, and—

DAYTON: That you would call CBS to suppress their news report?

MYERS: I called CBS to ask them to delay the

pictures showing on CBS' "60 Minutes" because I thought it would result in direct harm to our troops.

DAYTON: . . . Mr. Secretary, is that standard procedure for the military command of this country to try to suppress a news report at the highest level?

MYERS: It didn't—let me just—Senator Dayton, this is a serious allegation—

DAYTON: It sure is.

MYERS: —and it's absolutely—the context of your question I believe is wrong.[7]

In March 2004, more than 1,500 members and guests of the Radio and Television Correspondents Association attended its annual black-tie dinner, where President Bush entertained the throng with White House photographs showing him searching the nooks and crannies of the Oval Office for WMD and saying, "Nope, no weapons over there! Maybe under here?" The crowd roared with riotous laughter.[8]

In the months before the 2004 election, CBS News' *60 Minutes* produced but declined to air its investigation into the Niger forgeries claiming Saddam was seeking yellow uranium for nuclear

[7] Testimony before the Senate Armed Services Committee, May 7, 2004, http://findarticles.com/p/articles/mi_m0PAH/is_2004_May_7/ai_n6055221/pg_45.

[8] Sidney Blumenthal, *How Bush Rules: Chronicle of a Radical Regime* (Princeton: Princeton University Press, 2006), pp. 48–49.

weapons, a fabrication used as a central justification for war. Two years later, on the revamped *CBS Evening News*, the vituperative right-wing talk show host Rush Limbaugh, who had been fired from ESPN for inflammatory racial remarks, was invited to inaugurate its regular commentary on "civil discourse" (a segment the network soon canceled). And during the run-up to the 2006 midterm elections, ABC aired a two-part dramatization, supplied by right-wing partisans, of the terrorist attacks of September 11, 2001. The shows fabricated events and dialogue in order to cast blame on the Clinton administration and exonerate President Bush. Even though ABC executives were alerted beforehand to the falsified history, they chose to broadcast it anyway.

Meanwhile, the chairman of the Corporation for Public Broadcasting, overseeing the Public Broadcasting System, Kenneth Tomlinson, contracted a right-wing activist to investigate "liberal bias" at PBS. The CPB inspector general, however, reported that Tomlinson had imposed a "political test" on employees and hired favored consultants without properly informing the board. Tomlinson's crusade ended with his resignation in 2005.

The transactional nature of the Bush-era press corps surfaced in the 2007 trial of the vice president's chief of staff, *United States v. I. Lewis Libby*, when evidence of the administration's extensive manipulation of journalists was adjudicated under oath. The scandal began with a campaign ordered by Vice President Cheney to attempt to discredit former ambassador Joseph Wilson. After undertaking a mission for the CIA to ascertain whether Saddam Hussein was seeking yellowcake uranium in Niger, Wilson had found an utter absence of proof. In an op-ed article published in the *New York Times* in July 2003, he exposed as false President Bush's claim to that effect made in his 2003 State of the Union address—the president's most urgent reason for going to war. The White House tried to besmirch Wilson by prodding journalists to publish that his wife, Valerie Plame Wilson, an undercover CIA operative working on WMD, was responsible for sending him to Niger (a falsehood debunked in the trial).

Libby sought out Judith Miller, the *New York Times* reporter who the administration had used to plant the original disinformation about WMD, but, unbeknownst to Libby, Miller's editors had taken her off the beat. Karl Rove, the president's chief political adviser, spreading the smear, told a TV talk show host, "Wilson's wife is fair game."[9] Finally, conservative columnist Robert Novak exposed Plame's identity, despite having been

[9] Joseph Wilson, *The Politics of Truth: Inside the Lies that Put the White House on Trial and Betrayed My Wife's CIA Identity* (New York: Carroll & Graf, 2004), p. 1.

warned against doing so by the CIA's public affairs officer. Novak sent a copy of his prepublication column to Rove through a Republican lobbyist to let him know the hit was made.

More than a few members of the press had been recipients of the Plame leak from various White House aides, but they refused to disclose their sources, citing journalistic privilege. Miller went to jail for eighty-five days until she said her source, "Scooter" Libby, had released her from confidentiality. The court ruled against those journalists refusing to offer their testimony as witnesses to a crime, demolishing the customary journalistic privilege that actually had no standing in law but had received deference from government authorities until then. Libby claimed he had not been the source of the leak and repeatedly lied to the grand jury, saying that he had learned about Plame from journalists. After a trial featuring testimony from White House officials describing their techniques for exploiting the press, Libby was convicted on four counts of perjury and obstruction of justice.

•••

As Lippmann observed almost ninety years ago, the crisis of journalism cannot be disentangled from the crisis of national government. Government and journalism now share a crisis of credibility, trust, and competence. At the least, the crisis of journalism reveals a changing standard for and definition of "objectivity." Journalism, or more precisely, freedom of expression and freedom of the press, has been plunged, as a result of casual, callow, craven, or simply career-minded attitudes, into complicity, tacit and active, with a harsh and secretive administration that seeks to concentrate unaccountable power in the executive and sees itself as above the law and above reproach.

Only incidentally does the crisis of journalism involve the conflict between impartiality of judgment on the one hand and advocacy on the other. This might be a salient question under other circumstances, but it is peripheral here. Neither is the problem caused by slight inattentiveness; nor can it be solved by minor adjustments. The failure of most of the press for most of the Bush era to cover most of the basic reality was because to do so was too radical and threatening, not only to the administration but also to the news organizations themselves. Their dismal behavior goes to the root of a professional collapse. The press fiasco under Bush marks the culminating contradiction, if not repudiation, of Lippmann's original ideas about shaping journalistic standards for a modern age. It is not sheer happenstance, but the outcome of a long history that was by no means inevitable.

Two years after writing *Liberty and the News,*

Lippmann published *Public Opinion*, perhaps the most important book on American journalism in the twentieth century. It opened with an invocation, a long quotation from Plato's *Republic*, of the famous scene of cave dwellers who discern reality only as shadows dancing on the walls. Americans, Lippmann wrote, inhabited a cave of media misrepresentations of "the world outside," stereotypes, distortions of distortions—"not a mirror of social conditions, but the report of an aspect that has obtruded itself." Journalism became a media phantasmagoria, he wrote: "There are no objective standards here. There are conventions." He argued that a professional "intelligence bureau" of "expert reporters" that would present "a valid picture" of "the relevant environment" should be created, "interposing some form of expertness between the private citizen and the vast environment in which he is entangled." Disillusioned with politics, Lippmann turned to experts to act as arbiters of reality. He hoped that these antipolitical engineers would "disintegrate partisanship," establishing "footholds of reason." With that, Lippmann composed a Magna Carta for professional journalistic objectivity.

Gradually and imperceptibly, after taking decades to establish, the standard of objectivity shifted to become the opposite of what it had once been. Rather than serving as a method of describing the object, objectivity became an artificial balancing act of presenting competing claims about it. Objectivity turned into finding one hand and then the other hand, "fair and balanced," as the mocking slogan of Fox News put it. Editors, publishers, and other news executives often came to consider establishing the facts as untoward activism and advocacy. Fear of being accused of lacking "objectivity" drove them to bend over backward to demonstrate lack of bias by refusing to declare the facts themselves. Fairness was equated with lack of controversy. Objectivity became transformed from reporting into rationalizing the act of avoiding reporting. Professionalism, or expertise, as Lippmann understood it, was caricatured as a "liberal" ideological point of view—on the one hand—that must be balanced by another "conservative" ideological point of view—on the other hand. To the degree that this polarization became the standard, it successfully altered and neutered journalism. Professionalism receded in the name of professionalism.

Just as Lippmann's sense of objectivity took hold within the major news organizations by mid-century, the conservative movement began a counter trend. Objectivity was assailed as subjective, facts treated as opinion, reality as wholly ideological. Of course, during the New Deal and through the 1950s, most newspaper publishers were Republican, as they are today. But conservatives believed, nevertheless, that the new encroaching standards of objectivity in the major metropolitan press and national broadcast media reflected the power of a monolithic liberal establishment.

Richard Nixon turned his simmering resentment against "the establishment" into a focused strategy against the press. In November 1969, Vice President Spiro Agnew delivered a speech denouncing it as a "small [and] unelected elite." He warned, "The views of the majority of this fraternity do *not*—and I repeat, not—represent the views of America." And he even cited Walter Lippmann as an authority against "monopoly" over public opinion.[10]

After his landslide victory in 1972, Nixon urged the eccentric right-wing billionaire Richard Mellon Scaife to buy the *Washington Post*. Nixon's ploy launched Scaife on his subsequent crusade against "liberal media." In 1985, Scaife spent millions subsidizing a failed lawsuit by former general William Westmoreland against CBS News, trying to prove it had defamed him. (The same Scaife agents involved in that foray turned up later at the center of the $2.4 million Scaife-funded Arkansas Project of dirty tricks against President Clinton.)

As the Watergate scandal proved, Nixon's ef-

[10] David Brock, *The Republican Noise Machine* (New York: Three Rivers Press, 2005), pp. 25–27. For the text of Spiro Agnew's speech, see http://www.americanrhetoric.com/speeches/spiroagnewtvnews coverage.htm.

fort to demonize and isolate the press was part of his larger plan to formalize and institutionalize an imperial presidency. He sought an inherent power for the president to make war, declare national emergencies, nullify checks and balances by impounding funds at the president's discretion, create a system of secrecy, all rationalized by claims of national security. Checks and balances, oversight and accountability, exemplified by a rigorous press, were cast, following Agnew, as a fundamental threat to the country. From Nixon to George W. Bush, the impulse to build an unfettered executive has driven the essential struggle between the press and the presidency. The conservative movement's relentless campaign against "liberal bias" has been a lever to remove this check and balance.

The growth of a countervailing conservative media machine has also been a decisive political factor in mobilizing public opinion and insulating a part of it from contamination of "liberal bias." In October 2004, the University of Maryland Program on International Policy Attitudes conducted a study, "The Separate Realities of Bush and Kerry Supporters," revealing that 72 percent of Bush supporters believed that Saddam Hussein had WMD and that it had been proven, even though there had been extensive news reports from the Iraq Survey Group that it had found no WMD. Furthermore, 75 percent of Bush supporters believed that Saddam was substantially helping al Qaeda, 63 percent believed that that evidence had been found, 60 percent believed that experts agreed with that conclusion, and 55 percent believed that the 9/11 Commission had proven the point, even though it proved exactly the opposite. Bush supporters did not hold these misperceptions because of inattention to the news. Another University of Maryland study, "Misperceptions, the Media and the Iraq War," revealed that misperceptions varied significantly according to news sources and that higher levels of exposure to Fox News in particular compounded factual misperceptions and approval of Bush. Eighty percent of those who cited Fox News as a major source of their information suffered serious misperceptions, according to the study, compared to 23 percent citing National Public Radio and the Public Broadcasting System.[11]

"Without protection against propaganda, without standards of evidence, without criteria of emphasis, the living substance of all popular decision is exposed to every prejudice and to infinite

[11] University of Maryland Program on International Policy Attitudes, "The Separate Realities of Bush and Kerry Supporters," October 21, 2004, cited at http://www.worldpublicopinion.org/pipa/articles/united_statescanada_br/87.php?nid=&id=&pnt=87; "Misperceptions, the Media and the Iraq War," October 2, 2003, cited at http://www.worldpublicopinion.org/pipa/articles/international_security_bt/102.php?nid=&id=&pnt=102. Links to the full text of both studies can be found within the cited articles.

exploitation," Lippmann wrote in *Liberty and the News*. "The quack, the charlatan, the jingo, and the terrorist, can flourish only where the audience is deprived of independent access to information." Yet Lippmann assumed that the people were passive, acted upon by politically motivated elites. Today, about one-third of the public actively chooses sources of information that play to their prejudices. The readers, listeners, and viewers of the Drudge Report, the Rush Limbaugh show, and Fox News have consciously selected "the quack, the charlatan, the jingo" to seal themselves from objective information. The "breakdown of the means of public knowledge," as Lippmann called it, rests on a carefully cultivated preference for crank opinion over unsettling fact. The more reality defies this public's understanding, the more fervently it redoubles its resistance to it, embracing the distorted stereotype as the only true account.

The entrenchment and exploitation of this segment of public opinion has become big business and political necessity on the right. In May 2003, Matt Labash, a writer for the neoconservative journal *The Weekly Standard* (published by Rupert Murdoch, owner of Fox News), explained how the conservative attack on "liberal bias" operated as a profitable game. "While all these hand-wringing Freedom Forum types talk about objectivity, the conservative media likes to rap the liberal media on the knuckles for not being objective," he said. "We've created this cottage industry in which it pays to be un-objective. It pays to be subjective as much as possible. It's a great way to have your cake and eat it too. Criticize other people for not being objective. Be as subjective as you want. It's a great little racket. I'm glad we found it actually."[12]

The degree to which this "great little racket" has been accepted and assimilated by members of the press was expressed by Mark Halperin, then political editor of ABC News, in an appearance on a right-wing radio talk show in October 2006:

> Many people I work with in ABC, and other old media organizations, are liberal on a range of issues. And I think the ability of that, the reality of how that affects media coverage, is outrageous, and that conservatives in this country for forty years have felt that, and that it's something that must change. . . . And news organizations putting their heads in the sand for forty years, and not caring that half the country thought we were too liberal and biased against them was an insane business decision. But it was also insane to do from the point of view of what we're supposed to do as our core mission. . . . I don't know if it's 95% [the percentage of

[12] Interview with Matt Labash, May 2003, JournalismJobs.com, http://www.journalismjobs.com/matt_labash.cfm.

people with whom he works who are liberals],
and unfortunately, they're not all old. There
are a lot of young liberals here, too. But it certainly, there are enough in the old media, not
just in ABC, but in old media generally, that it
tilts the coverage quite frequently, in many issues, in a liberal direction, which is completely
improper.[13]

"From our recent experience," wrote Lippmann, "it is clear that the traditional liberties of
speech and opinion rest on no solid foundation."
Journalism must reconstruct itself for a new age,
at least as urgently as in Lippmann's time. So far
it has failed the tests of the new century. Nearly
ninety years after Lippmann first assayed the crisis of journalism, it finds itself back at ground
zero—or in Lippmann's cave. Even some of the
impassioned amateurs of the Internet have been
more factually reliable on central issues than the
most august news organizations. Their fear—as
readers, viewers, and influence seep away in the
face of new technology—has provoked more anx-
iety than self-examination. But journalism may
yet be revitalized, as part of a general reawaken-
ing of American democracy that discovers new

[13] Interview with Mark Halperin, October 30, 2006, *The Hugh
Hewitt Show*, a transcript of which can be found at http://hugh
hewitt.townhall.com/Transcript_Page.aspx?ContentGuid=1f13356
2-cfd3-40f8-af2f-129219d59c8d.

forms of expression and forces new debate to achieve its ends.

The filigree of wire, cathode-ray tubes, woofers and tweeters, satellite dishes, and printing presses are the same everywhere in a flat world. But Americans are wired differently. The freedom of the press is part of our Constitution, the first right, the First Amendment; and our democracy—public policy, politics, commerce, and nation—has been shaped by its exercise, its use, and its abuse.

In 1822, in a placid time, an "Era of Good Feelings," as it was called, James Madison was nonetheless eternally vigilant about liberty and the news. "A popular Government without popular information, or the means of acquiring it, is but a Prologue to a Farce or a Tragedy, or perhaps both," he wrote. "Knowledge will forever govern ignorance, and a people who mean to be their own Governors, must arm themselves with the power which knowledge gives."

Index